S0-CPS-143

Love's Coming-of-Age

LOVE'S COMING OF AGE

By EDWARD CARPENTER

BONI AND LIVERIGHT, INC.

PUBLISHERS .·. .·. NEW YORK

PREFATORY NOTE BY THE AUTHOR

When I first wrote this book some fifteen years ago, it was refused in succession by five or six well-known London publishers; and ultimately I had to print it at my own expense. Such was the taboo then prevailing on matters of sex. To-day, however, the book is translated into many European languages, and in Germany has reached its fourteenth or fifteenth edition. And to-day people are beginning to see that a decent and straightforward discussion of sex-questions is not only permissible, but is quite necessary, if ever we are to have a better order in this department of human life.

The present edition is the only specially authorized American issue, and contains all the latest additions and corrections up to date.

EDWARD CARPENTER.

April, 1911.

LOVE'S COMING-OF-AGE

Love's Coming-of-Age

THE SEX-PASSION

THE subject of Sex is difficult to deal with. There is no doubt a natural reticence connected with it. There is also a great deal of prudery. The passion occupies, without being spoken of, a large part of human thought; and words on the subject being so few and inadequate, everything that *is* said is liable to be misunderstood. Violent inferences are made and equivocations surmised, from the simplest remarks; qualified admissions of liberty are interpreted into recommendations of unbridled license; and generally the perspective of literary expression is turned upside down.

There is, in fact, a vast deal of fetishism in the current treatment of the question. Nor can one altogether be surprised at this when one sees how important Sex is in the scheme of things, and how deeply it has been associated since the earliest times not only with man's personal impulses, but even with his religious sentiments and ceremonials.

Next to hunger it is doubtless the most primitive and imperative of our needs. But in modern civilised life Sex enters probably even more into *consciousness* than hunger. For the hunger-needs of the human race are in the later societies fairly well satisfied, but the sex-desires are strongly restrained, both by law and custom, from satisfaction—and so assert themselves all the more in thought.

To find the place of these desires, their utterance, their control, their personal import, their social import, is a tremendous problem to every youth and girl, man and woman.

There are a few of both sexes, doubtless, who hardly feel the passion—who have never been "in love," and who experience no strong sexual appetite—but these are rare. Practically the passion is a matter of universal experience; and speaking broadly and generally we may say it is a matter on which it is quite desirable that every adult at some time or other *should* have actual experience. There may be exceptions; but, as said, the instinct lies so deep and is so universal, that for the understanding of life—of one's own life, of that of others, and of human nature in general—as well as for the proper development of one's own capacities, such experience is as a rule needed.

And here in passing I would say that in the social life of the future this need will surely be recognised, and that (while there will be no stigma attaching to voluntary celibacy) the state of enforced celibacy in which vast numbers of women live to-day will be looked upon as a national wrong, almost as grievous as that of prostitution —of which latter evil indeed it is in some degree the counterpart or necessary accompaniment.

Of course Nature (personifying under this term the more unconscious, even though human, instincts and forces) takes pretty good care in her own way that sex shall not be neglected. She has her own purposes to work out, which in a sense have nothing to do with the individual—her racial purposes. But she acts in the rough, with tremendous sweep and power, and with little adjustment to or consideration for the later developed and more conscious and intelligent ideals of humanity. The youth, deeply infected with the sex-passion, suddenly finds himself in the presence of Titanic forces—the Titanic but sub-conscious forces of his own nature. "In love" he feels a superhuman impulse—and naturally so, for he identifies himself with cosmic energies and entities, powers that are preparing the future of the race, and whose operations extend over vast regions of space and millennial lapses of time. He sees into the abysmal depths of his own being, and trembles with a kind of awe at the disclosure. And what he feels concerning himself he feels similarly concerning the one who has inspired his passion. The glances of the two lovers penetrate far beyond the surface, ages down into each other, waking a myriad antenatal dreams.

For the moment he lets himself go, rejoicing in the sense of limitless power beneath him—borne onwards like a man down rapids, too intoxicated with the glory of motion to think of whither he is going; then the next moment he discovers that he is being hurried into impossible situations—situations which his own moral conscience, as well as the moral conscience of Society, embodied in law and custom, will not admit. He finds perhaps that the satisfaction of his imperious impulse is, to all appearances, inconsistent with the welfare of her he loves. His own passion arises before him as a kind of rude giant which he or the race to which he belongs may, Frankenstein-like, have created ages back, but which he now has to dominate or be dominated by; and there declares itself in him the fiercest conflict—that between his far-back Titanic instinctive and sub-conscious nature, and his later developed, more especially human and moral self.

While the glory of Sex pervades and suffuses all Nature; while the flowers are rayed and starred out towards the sun in the very ecstasy of generation; while the nostrils of the animals dilate, and their forms become instinct, under the passion, with a proud and fiery beauty; while even the human lover is transformed, and in the great splendors of the mountains and the sky perceives something to which he had not the key before—yet it is curious that just here, in Man, we find the magic wand of Nature suddenly broken, and doubt and conflict and division entering in, where a kind of unconscious harmony had erst prevailed.

And the reason of this is not far to seek. For in comparing, as we did a page or two back, the sex-needs and the hunger-needs of the human race, we left out of account one great difference, namely that while food (the object of hunger) has no moral rights of its own,* and can be appropriated without misgiving on that score, the object of sex is a person, and cannot be used for private advantage without the most dire infringement of the law of equality. The moment Man rises into any sort of consciousness of the equal rights of others with himself his love-needs open

* Though this is of course not true of *animal* food.

up this terrible problem. His needs are no less —perhaps they are greater—than they were before, but they are stricken with a deadly swound at the thought that there is something even greater than them.

Heine, I think, says somewhere that the man who loves unsuccessfully knows himself to be a god. It is not perhaps till the great current of sexual love is checked and brought into conflict with the other parts of his being that the whole nature of the man, sexual and moral, under the tremendous stress rises into consciousness and reveals in fire its god-like quality. This is the work of the artificer who makes immortal souls—who out of the natural love evolves even a more perfect love. "In tutti gli amanti," says Giordano Bruno, "è questo fabro vulcano" ("in all lovers is this Olympian blacksmith present").

It is the subject of this conflict, or at least differentiation, between the sexual and the more purely moral and social instincts in man which interests us here. It is clear, I think, that if sex is to be treated rationally, that is, neither superstitiously on the one hand nor licentiously on the other, we must be willing to admit that both the satisfaction of the passion and the non-satisfaction of it are desirable and beautiful. They both have their results, and man has to reap the fruits which belong to both experiences. May we not say that there is probably some sort of Transmutation of essences continually effected and effectible in the human frame? Lust and Love—the *Aphrodite Pandemos* and the *Aphrodite Ouranios* —are subtly interchangeable. Perhaps the corporeal amatory instinct and the ethereal human yearning for personal union are really and in essence one thing with diverse forms of manifestation. However that may be, it is pretty evident that there is *some* deep relationship between them. It is a matter of common experience that the unrestrained outlet of merely physical desire leaves the nature drained of its higher love-forces; while on the other hand if the physical satisfaction be denied, the body becomes surcharged with waves of emotion—sometimes to an unhealthy and dangerous degree. Yet at times this emotional love may, by reason of its expression being checked or restricted, transform itself into the all-penetrating subtle influence of spiritual love.

Marcus Aurelius quotes a saying of Heraclitus to the effect that the death of earth is to become water (liquefaction), and the death of water is to become air (evaporation), and the death of air is to become fire (combustion). So in the human body are there sensual, emotional, spiritual, and other elements of which it may be said that their death on one plane means their transformation and new birth on other planes.

It will readily be seen that I am not arguing that the lower or more physical manifestations of love should be killed out in order to force the growth of the more spiritual and enduring forms —because Nature in her slow evolutions does not generally countenance such high and mighty methods; but am merely trying to indicate that there are grounds for believing in the transmutability of the various forms of the passion, and grounds for thinking that the sacrifice of a lower phase may sometimes be the only condition on which a higher and more durable phase can be attained; and that therefore Restraint (which is absolutely necessary at times) *has* its compensation.

Any one who has once realised how glorious a thing Love is in its essence, and how indestructible, will hardly need to call anything that leads to it a sacrifice; and he is indeed a master of life who, accepting the grosser desires as they come to his body, and not refusing them, knows how to transform them at will into the most rare and fragrant flowers of human emotion.

Until these subjects are openly put before children and young people with some degree of intelligent and sympathetic handling, it can scarcely be expected that anything but the utmost confusion, in mind and morals, should reign in matters of Sex. That we should leave our children to pick up their information about the most sacred, the most profound and vital, of all human functions, from the mere gutter, and learn to know it first from the lips of ignorance and vice, seems almost incredible, and certainly indicates the deeply-rooted unbelief and uncleanliness of our own thoughts. Yet a child at the age of puberty, with the unfolding of its far-down emotional and sexual nature, is eminently capable of the most sensitive, affectional, and serene appreciation of what Sex means (generally more so, as things are to-day, than its worldling parent or guardian); and can absorb the teaching, if sympathetically given, without any shock or disturbance to its sense of shame—that sense which is so natural and valuable a safeguard of early youth. To teach the child first, quite openly, its physical relation to its own mother, its long indwelling in her body, and the deep and sacred bond of tenderness between mother and child in consequence; then, after a time, to explain the relation of fatherhood, and how the love of the parents for each other was the cause of its own (the child's) existence: these things are easy and natural—at least they are so to the young mind—and excite in it no surprise, or sense of unfitness, but only gratitude and a kind of tender wonderment.* Then, later on, as the special sexual needs and desires develop, to instruct the girl or boy in the further details of the matter, and the care and right conduct of her or his own sexual nature; on the meaning and the dangers of solitary indulgence—if this habit has been contracted; on the need of self-control and the presence of affection in all relations with others, and (without undue asceticism) on the possibility of deflecting physical desire to some degree into affectional and emotional channels, and the great gain so resulting; all these are things which an ordinary youth of either sex will easily understand and appreciate, and which may be of priceless value, saving such an one from years of struggle in foul morasses, and waste of precious life-strength. Finally, with the maturity of the moral nature, the supremacy of the pure human relation should be taught—not the extinguishment of desire, but the attainment of the real kernel of it, its dedication to the well-being of another—the evolution of the *human* element in love, balancing the natural—till at last the snatching of an unglad pleasure, regardless of the other from whom it is snatched, or the surrender of one's body to another, for any reason except that of love, become things impossible.

---

* *See* "Appendix."

Between lovers then a kind of hardy temperance is much to be recommended—for all reasons, but especially because it lifts their satisfaction and delight in each other out of the region of ephemeralities (which too soon turn to dull indifference and satiety) into the region of more lasting things—one step nearer at any rate to the Eternal Kingdom. How intoxicating indeed, how penetrating—like a most precious wine—is that love which is the sexual transformed by the magic of the will into the emotional and spiritual! And what a loss on the merest grounds of prudence and the economy of pleasure is its unbridled waste along physical channels! So nothing is so much to be dreaded between lovers as just this—the vulgarisation of love—and this is the rock upon which marriage so often splits.

There is a kind of illusion about physical desire similar to that which a child suffers from when, seeing a beautiful flower, it instantly snatches the same, and destroys in a few moments the form and fragrance which attracted it. He only gets the full glory who holds himself back a little, and truly possesses who is willing if need be not to possess.

On the other hand it must not be pretended that the physical passions are by their nature unclean, or otherwise than admirable and desirable in their place. Any attempt to absolutely disown or despite them, carried out over long periods either by individuals or bodies of people, only ends in the *thinning out* of the human nature—by the very consequent stinting of the supply of its growth-material, and is liable to stultify itself in time by leading to reactionary excesses. It must never be forgotten that the physical basis throughout life is of the first importance, and supplies the nutrition and food-stuff without which the higher powers cannot exist or at least manifest themselves. Intimacies founded on intellectual and moral affinities alone are seldom very deep and lasting; if the physical basis in any form is quite absent, the acquaintanceship is liable to die away again like an ill-rooted plant. In many cases (especially of women) the nature is never really understood or disclosed till the sex feeling is touched—however lightly. Besides it must be remembered that in order for a perfect intimacy between two people their bodies must by the nature of the case be free to each other. The bodily intimacy or endearment may not be the object for which they come together; but if it is denied, its denial will bar any real sense of repose and affiance, and make the relation restless, vague, tentative and unsatisfied.

In these lights it will be seen that what we call

asceticism and what we call libertinism are two sides practically of the same shield. So long as the tendency towards mere pleasure-indulgence is strong and uncontrolled, so long will the instinct towards asceticism assert itself—and rightly, else we might speedily find ourselves in headlong Phaethonian career. Asceticism is in its place (as the word would indicate) as an *exercise;* but let it not be looked upon as an end in itself, for that is a mistake of the same kind as going to the opposite extreme. Certainly if the welfare and happiness of the beloved one were always really the main purpose in our minds we should have plenty of occasion for self-control, and an artificial asceticism would not be needed. We look for a time doubtless when the hostility between these two parts of man's unperfected nature will be merged in the perfect love; but at present and until this happens their conflict is certainly one of the most pregnant things in all our experience; and must not by any means be blinked or evaded, but boldly faced. It is in itself almost a sexual act. The mortal nature through it is, so to speak, torn asunder; and through the rent so made in his mortality does it sometimes happen that a new and immortal man is born.

Sex-pleasures afford a kind of type of all pleasure. The dissatisfaction which at times follows on them is the same as follows on all pleasure which is *sought*, and which does not come unsought. The dissatisfaction is not in the nature of pleasure itself, but in the nature of *seeking*. In going off in pursuit of things external, the "I" (since it really has everything and needs nothing) deceives itself, goes out from its true home, tears itself asunder, and admits a gap or rent in its own being. This, it must be supposed, is what is meant by *sin*—the separation or sundering of one's being—and all the pain that goes therewith. It all consists in *seeking* those external things and pleasures; not (a thousand times be it said) in the external things or pleasures themselves. They are all fair and gracious enough; their place is to stand round the throne and offer their homage —rank behind rank in their multitudes—if so be we will accept it. But for us to go out of ourselves to run after *them*, to allow ourselves to be divided and rent in twain by *their* attraction, that is an inversion of the order of heaven.

To this desertion of one's true self sex tempts most strongly, and stands as the type of Maya and the world-illusion; yet the beauty of the loved one and the delight of corporeal union all turn to dust and ashes if bought at the price of disunion and disloyalty in the higher spheres—disloyalty even to the person whose mortal love is sought. The higher and more durable part of man, whirled along in the rapids and whirlpools of desire, experiences tortures the moment it comes to recognise that It is something other than physical. Then comes the struggle to regain its lost Paradise, and the frightful effort of co-ordination between the two natures, by which the centre of consciousness is gradually transferred from the fugitive to the more permanent part, and the mortal and changeable is assigned its due place in the outer chambers and forecourts of the temple.

Pleasure should come as the natural (and indeed inevitable) accompaniment of life, believed in with a kind of free faith, but never sought as the object of life. It is in the inversion of this order that the uncleanness of the senses arises. Sex to-day throughout the domains of civilisation is thoroughly unclean. Everywhere it is slimed over with the thought of pleasure. Not for joy, not for mere delight in and excess of life, not for pride in the generation of children, not for a symbol and expression of deepest soul-union, does it exist—but for our own gratification. Hence we disown it in our thoughts, and cover it up with false shame and unbelief—knowing well that to seek a social act for a private end is a falsehood. The body itself is kept religiously covered, smothered away from the rush of the great purifying life of Nature, infected with dirt and disease, and a subject for prurient thought and exaggerated lust such as in its naked state it would never provoke. The skin becomes sickly and corrupt, and of a dead leaden white hue, which strangely enough is supposed to be more beautiful than the rich rose-brown, delicately shaded into lighter tints in the less exposed parts, which it would wear if tanned by daily welcome of sun and wind. Sexual embraces themselves seldom receive the benison of Dame Nature, in whose presence alone, under the burning sun or the high canopy of the stars and surrounded by the fragrant atmosphere, their meaning can be fully understood: but take place in stuffy dens of dirty upholstery and are associated with all unbeautiful things.

Even literature, which might have been expected to preserve some decent expression on this topic, reflects all too clearly by its silence or by its pruriency the prevailing spirit of unbelief; and in order to find any sane, faithful, strong, and calm words on the subject, one has to wade right back through the marshes and bogs of civilised scribbledom, and toil eastward across its arid wastes to the very dawn-hymns of the Aryan races.

In one of the Upanishads of the Vedic sacred books (the Brihadaranyaka Upanishad) there is a fine passage in which instruction is given to the man who desires a noble son as to the prayers which he shall offer to the gods on the occasion of congress with his wife. In primitive simple and serene language it directs him, how at such times, he should pray to the various forms of deity who preside over the operations of Nature: to Vishnu to prepare the womb of the future mother, to Prajápati to watch over the influx of the semen, and to the other gods to nourish the fœtus, etc. Nothing could be (I am judging from the only translation I have met with, a Latin one) more composed, serene, simple, and religious in feeling, and well might it be if such instructions were preserved and followed, even to-day; yet such is the pass we have come to that actually Max Müller in his translations of the Sacred Books of the East appears to have been unable to persuade himself to render these and a few other quite similar passages into English, but gives them in the original Sanskrit! One might have thought that as Professor in the University of Oxford, presumedly *sans peur et sans reproche*, and professedly engaged in making a translation of these books for students, it was his duty and it might have been his delight to make intelligible just such passages as these, which give the pure and pious sentiment of the early world in so perfect a form; unless indeed he thought the sentiment impure and impious—in which case we have indeed a measure of the degradation of the public opinion which must have swayed his mind. As to the only German translation of the Upanishad which I can find, it baulks at the same passages in the same feeble way—repeating *nicht wiederzugeben, nicht wiederzugeben,* over and over again, till at last one can but conclude that the translator is right, and that the simplicity and sacredness of the feeling is in this our time indeed "not to be reproduced."

Our public opinion, our literature, our customs, our laws, are saturated with the notion of the uncleanness of Sex, and are so making the conditions of its cleanness more and more difficult. Our children, as said, have to pick up their intelligence on the subject in the gutter. Little boys bathing on the outskirts of our towns are hunted down by idiotic policemen, apparently infuriated by the sight of the naked body, even of childhood. Lately in one of our northern towns, the boys and men bathing in a public pool set apart by the corporation for the purpose, were—though forced to wear some kind of covering—kept till nine o'clock at night before they were allowed to go into the water—lest in the full daylight Mrs. Grundy should behold any portion of their bodies! and as for women and girls their disabilities in the matter are most serious.

Till this dirty and dismal sentiment with regard to the human body is removed there can be little hope of anything like a free and gracious public life. With the regeneration of our social ideas the whole conception of Sex as a thing covert and to be ashamed of, marketable and unclean, will have to be regenerated. That inestimable freedom and pride which is the basis of all true manhood and womanhood will have to enter into this most intimate relation to preserve it frank and pure—pure from the damnable commercialism which buys and sells all human things, and from the religious hypocrisy which covers and conceals; and a healthy delight in and cultivation of the body and all its natural functions, and a determination to keep them pure and beautiful, open and sane and free, will have to become a recognised part of national life.

Possibly, and indeed probably, as the sentiment of common life and common interest grows, and the capacity for true companionship increases with the decrease of self-regarding anxiety, the importance of the mere sex-act will dwindle till it comes to be regarded as only one very specialised factor in the full total of human love. There is no doubt that with the full realisation of affectional union the need of the actual bodily congress loses some of its urgency; and it is not difficult to see in our present-day social life that the want of the former is (according to the law of transmutation) one marked cause of the violence and extravagance of the lower passions. But however things may change with the further evolution of man, there is no doubt that first of all the sex-relation must be divested of the sentiment of uncleanness which surrounds it, and rehabilitated again with a sense almost of religious consecration; and this means, as I have said, a free people, proud in the mastery and the divinity of their own lives, and in the beauty and openness of their own bodies.*

Sex is the allegory of love in the physical world. It is from this fact that it derives its immense power. The aim of Love is non-differentiation—absolute union of being; but absolute union can only be found at the centre of existence. Therefore whoever has truly found another has found not only that other, and with that other himself, but has found also a third—who dwells at the centre and holds the plastic

---

* *See* "Appendix."

material of the universe in the palm of his hand, and is a creator of sensible forms.

Similarly the aim of sex is union and non-differentiation—but on the physical plane,—and in the moment when this union is accomplished creation takes place, and the generation (in the plastic material of the sex-elements) of sensible forms.

In the animal and lower human world—and wherever the creature is incapable of realising the perfect love (which is indeed able to transform it into a god)—Nature in the purely physical instincts does the next best thing, that is, she effects a corporeal union and so generates another creature who by the very process of his generation shall be one step nearer to the universal soul and the realisation of the desired end. Nevertheless the moment the other love and all that goes with it is realised the natural sexual love has to fall into a secondary place—the lover must stand on his feet and not on his head—or else the most dire confusions ensue, and torments æonian.

Taking all together I think it may fairly be said that the prime object of Sex is *union*, the physical union as the allegory and expression of the real union, and that generation is a secondary object or result of this union. If we go to the lowest material expressions of Sex—as among the protozoic cells—we find that they, the cells, unite together, two into one; and that, as a result of the nutrition that ensues, this joint cell after a time (but not always) breaks up by fission into a number of progeny cells; or if on the other hand we go to the very highest expression of Sex, in the sentiment of Love, we find the latter takes the form chiefly and before all else of a desire for union, and only in lesser degree of a desire for race-propagation.*

I mention this because it probably makes a good deal of difference in our estimate of Sex whether the one function or the other is considered primary. There is perhaps a slight tendency among medical and other authorities to overlook the question of the important physical actions and reactions, and even corporeal modifications, which may ensue upon sexual intercourse between two people, and to fix their attention too exclusively upon their child-bearing function; but in truth it is probable, I think, from various con-

* Taking union as the main point we may look upon the idealised Sex-love as a sense of contact pervading the whole mind and body—while the sex-organs are a specialisation of this faculty of union in the outermost sphere: union in the bodily sphere giving rise to bodily generation, the same as union in the mental and emotional spheres occasions generation of another kind.

siderations,† that the spermatozoa pass through the tissues and affect the general body of the female, as well as that the male absorbs minutest cells *from* the female; and that generally, even without the actual Sex-act, there is an interchange of vital and ethereal elements—so that it might be said there is a kind of generation taking place *within* each of the persons concerned, through their mutual influence on each other, as well as that more specialised generation which consists in the propagation of the race.

At the last and taking it as a whole one has the same difficulty in dealing with the subject of Love which meets one at every turn in modern life—the monstrous separation of one part of our nature from another—the way in which, no doubt in the necessary course of evolution, we have cut ourselves in twain as it were, and assigned "right" and "wrong," heaven and hell, spiritual and material, and other violent distinctions, to the separate portions. We have eaten of the Tree of Knowledge of good and evil with a vengeance!

† These are (1) the curious, not yet explained, facts of "Telegony"—*i.e.*, the tendency (often noticed in animals) of the children of a dam by a second sire to resemble the first sire; (2) the probable survival, in a modified form, of the primitive close relation (as seen in the protozoa) between copulation and nutrition; (3) the great activity of the spermatozoa themselves.

The Lord has indeed driven us out of Paradise into the domain of that "fabro vulcano" who with tremendous hammer-strokes must *hammer the knowledge of good and evil out of us again.* I feel that I owe an apology to the beautiful god for daring even for a moment to think of dissecting him soul from body, and for speaking as if these artificial distinctions were in any wise eternal. Will the man or woman, or race of men and women, never come, to whom love in its various manifestations shall be from the beginning a perfect whole, pure and natural, free and standing sanely on its feet?

MAN

THE UNGROWN

MAN, the ordinary human male, is a curious animal. While mastering the world with his pluck, skill, enterprise, he is in matters of Love for the most part a child. The passion plays havoc with him; nor does he ride the Leopard, as Ariadne is fabled to have done.

In this he differs from the other sex; and the difference can be seen in earliest years. When the boy is on his rocking horse, the girl is caressing her doll. When the adolescent youth, burning to master a real quadruped, is still somewhat contemptuous of Love's power, "sweet seventeen" has already lost and regained her heart several times, and is accomplished in all the finesse of feeling.

To the grown man love remains little more than a plaything. Affairs, politics, fighting, money-making, creative art, constructive industry, are his serious business; the affections are his relaxation; passion is the little fire with which he toys, and which every now and then flares out and burns him up. His affections, his passions, are probably as a rule stronger than woman's; but he never attains to understand them or be master of their craft. With woman all this is reversed.

A man pelts along on his hobby—his business, his career, his latest invention, or what not—forgetful that there is such a thing in the world as the human heart; then all of a sudden he "falls in love," tumbles headlong in the most ludicrous way, fills the air with his cries, struggles frantically like a fly in treacle: and all the time hasn't the faintest idea whether he has been inveigled into the situation, or whether he got there of his own accord, or what he wants now he is there. Suicides, broken hearts, lamentations, and certainly a whole panorama, marvellous in beauty, of lyrical poetry and art, mark the experience of love's distress in Man. Woman in the same plight neither howls nor cries, she does not commit suicide or do anything extravagant, she creates not a single poem or work of art of any account; but she simply goes her way and suffers in silence, shaping her life to the new conditions. Never for a moment does she forget that her one serious object is Love; but never for a moment does she "give herself away" or lose her head, in the pursuit of that object.

It is perhaps a kind of revenge for this that man for so many centuries has made woman his serf. Feeling that she really somehow mastered him on the affectional plane, he in revenge on the physical plane has made the most of his superior strength, and of his power over her; or, more probably, not thinking about it at all, he has simply allowed all along the sex-passion (so strong in him) to prompt him to this mastery.

For the sex-passion in man is undoubtedly a force—huge and fateful—which has to be reckoned with. Perhaps (speaking broadly) *all* the passions and powers, the intellect and affections and emotions and all, are really profounder and vaster in Man than in Woman—are more varied, root deeper, and have wider scope; but then the woman has this advantage, that her powers are more co-ordinated, are in harmony with each other, where his are disjointed or in conflict. A girl comes of age sooner than a boy. And the coming-of-age of Love (which harmonises all the faculties in the human being) may take place early in the woman, while in the man it is delayed long and long, perhaps never completely effected. The problem is so much bigger, so much more complex, with him; it takes longer for its solution. Women are sometimes impatient with men on this score; but then they do not see, judging from their own little flock, what a big herd of cattle the man has to bring home.

Anyhow, the point is that Man with his great uncoördinated nature *has* during these later centuries dominated the other sex, and made himself the ruler of society. In consequence of which we naturally have a society made after his pattern—a society advanced in mechanical and intellectual invention, with huge passional and emotional elements, but all involved in whirling confusion and strife—a society ungrown, which on its material side may approve itself a great success, but on its more human and affectional side seems at times an utter failure.

This ungrown, half-baked sort of character is conspicuous in the class of men who organise the modern world—the men of the English-speaking, well-to-do class. The boy of this class begins life at a public school. He does not learn much from the masters; but he knocks about among his fellows in cricket and football and athletics, and turns out with an excellent organising capacity and a tolerably firm and reliable grip on the practical and material side of life—qualities which are of first-rate importance, and which give the English ruling classes a similar mission in the world to the Romans of the early Empire. A certain standard too (for what it is worth) of schoolboy honor and fairness is thumped into him. It is very narrow and conventional, but at its best rises as high as a conception of self-sacrifice and duty, though never to the conception of love. At the same time a strong and lavish diet and an easy life stimulate his functional energies and his animal passions to a high degree.

Here certainly is some splendid material, and if well pounded into shape, kneaded and baked, might result in a useful upper crust for society. But alas! it remains, or actually degenerates into, a most fatuous dough. The boy never learns anything after he leaves school. He gets no more thumps. He glides easily into the higher walks of the world—backed by his parents' money—into Law or Army or Church or Civil Service or Commerce. He has really no serious fights to fight, or efforts to make, sees next to nothing of actual life; has an easy time, can marry pretty well whom he chooses, or console himself with unmarried joys; and ultimately settles down into the routine and convention of his particular profession—a picture of beefy self-satisfaction. Affection and tenderness of feeling, though latent in him, have never, owing to the unfortunate conditions of his life, been developed; but their place begins to be taken by a rather dreary cynicism. Sex, always strong, still even now in its waning days, retains the first place; and the mature man, having no adequate counterpoise to it in the growth of his sympathetic nature, is fain to find his highest restraints or sanctions in the unripe code of his school-days or the otiose conventions and prejudices of the professional clique to which he belongs.

So it comes about that the men who have the sway of the world to-day are in the most important matters quite ungrown; they really have never come of age in any adequate sense. Like Ephraim they are "a cake not turned." Wherever they turn up: in Lords or Commons, Civil or Military, Law or Church or Medicine, the Judge on the bench, the Bishop, the ruler of India, the exploiter of South Africa, the man who booms a company in the city, or who builds up a great commercial trust and gets a title for supporting a Government, it is much the same. Remove the distinctive insignia of their clique and office, and you find underneath—no more than a public school-boy. Perhaps, indeed, rather less; for while the school-boy mind is there, and the school-boy code of life and honor, the enthusiasm and the promise of youth are gone.

It is certainly very maddening at times to think that the Destinies of the world, the organisation of society, the wonderful scope of possible statesmanship, the mighty issues of trade and industry, the loves of Women, the lives of criminals, the fate of savage nations, should be in the hands of such a set of general nincompoops; men so fatuous that it actually does not hurt them to see the streets crammed with prostitutes by night, or the parks by day with the semi-lifeless bodies of tramps; men, to whom it seems quite natural that our marriage and social institutions should lumber along over the bodies of women, as our commercial institutions grind over the bodies of the poor, and our "imperial" enterprise over the bodies of barbarian races, destroyed by drink and devilry. But then no doubt the world is made like that. Assuredly it is no wonder that the more go-ahead Women (who have come round to the light by their own way, and through much darkness and suffering) should rise in revolt; or that the Workmen (finding their lives in the hands of those who do not know what life is) should do the same.

Leaving now the Middle-class man of to-day, the great representative of modern civilisation, and the triumphant outcome of so many centuries of human progress, to enjoy his distinctions—we may turn for a moment to the only other great body of men who are of any importance: the more capable and energetic manual workers.

In the man of this class we have a type superior

in many ways to the other. In the first place he knows something of what Life is; from an early age probably he has had to do something towards his own living. Anyhow he has been called upon in a thousand ways to help his parents, or his brothers and sisters, and has developed a fair capacity of sympathy and affection—a thing which can hardly be said of the public school-boy; while his work, narrow though it may be, has given him a certain definite ability and grasp of actual fact. If, as is now happening in hundreds of thousands of cases, there is superadded to all this some of the general culture which arises from active reading and study, it is clear that the result is going to be considerable. It may not count much to-day, but it will to-morrow.

On the other hand this class is lamentably wanting in the very point where the other man excels—the organising faculty. Take a workman from the bench, where he has never so to speak had to look beyond his nose, and place him in a position of responsibility and command, and he is completely at sea. He turns out hopelessly slattern and ineffectual, or a martinet or a bully; he has no sense of perspective and stickles absurdly over little points while he lets the great ones go; and it is almost impossible for him to look before and after as he should do, or bring to a proper focus a whole field of considerations. In all this he is a mere child: and evidently by himself unfit to rule the world.

In many respects the newer Women and the Workmen resemble each other. Both have been bullied and sat upon from time immemorial, and are beginning to revolt; both are good at detailed and set or customary work, both are bad at organisation; both are stronger on the emotional than on the intellectual side; and both have an ideal of better things, but do not quite see their way to carry it out. Their best hope, perhaps, lies in their both getting hold of the Middle-class Man and thumping him on each side till they get him to organise the world for them. The latter has no ideal, no object, no enthusiasm of his own. He cannot set himself to work; and consequently he is just made use of by the commercial spirit of the day. It is really lamentable to think how his great organising capacity—which might create a holy Human empire of the world—is simply at present the tool of the Jew and the Speculator. In Parliamentary, Military, Indian, Home or Colonial politics, the quondam public school-boy is just led by the nose by the money-grubbing interest, to serve its purposes; and half the time has not the sense to see that he is being so led.

It might seem that it would be the greatest

blessing and benefit to the man of this class to find him an ideal to work to. Certainly it is his only real and conceivable function to form an alliance with the two other great classes of the modern nations—the women and the workmen—and organise for them. Whether he will see it so, we know not; but if this might come about great things would happen in the world.

WOMAN

THE SERF

A HALF-GROWN man is of course a tyrant. And so it has come about that the rule of Man in the world has for many ages meant the serfdom of Woman.

Far back in History, at a time when in the early societies the thought of inequality had hardly arisen, it would appear that the female in her own way—as sole authenticator of birth and parentage, as guardian of the household, as inventress of agriculture and the peaceful arts, as priestess or prophetess or sharer in the councils of the tribe—was as powerful as man in his, and sometimes even more so. But from thence, down to to-day, what centuries of repression, of slavehood, of dumbness and obscurity have been her lot!

There is much to show that the greed of Private Property was the old Serpent which brought about the fall of our first parents; for as this sentiment—the chief incentive to modern Civilisation—rose and spread with a kind of contagion over the advancing races of mankind, the human

Male, bitten by it, not only claimed possession of everything he could lay hands upon, but ended by enslaving and appropriating his own mate, his second self—reducing her also to a mere chattel, a slave and a plaything.

Certainly it is curious that, with whatever occasional exceptions, the periods of man's ascendancy have been the periods of so much sadness and degradation of women. He, all through, more and more calmly assuming that it must be her province to live and work for him; shutting her more and more into the seclusion of the boudoir and the harem, or down to the drudgery of the hearth; confining her body, her mind; playing always upon her sex-nature, accentuating always that—as though she were indeed nought else but sex; yet furious if her feelings were not always obedient to his desire; arrogating to himself a masculine licence, yet revenging the least unfaithfulness on her part by casting her out into the scorned life of the prostitute; and granting her more and more but one choice in life—to be a free woman, and to die, unsexed, in the gutter; or for creature-comforts and a good name to sell herself, soul and body, into life-long bondage. While she, more and more, has accepted as inevitable the situation; and moved, sad-eyed, to her patient and uncomplaining work, to the narrow sphere and petty details of household labor and life, of patience and self-effacement, of tenderness and love, little noticed and less understood; or twisted herself into a ridiculous mime of fashion and frivolity, if so she might find a use for her empty head, and some favor with her lord; her own real impulses and character, her own talents and genius, all the while smothered away and blighted, her brain dwarfed, and her outlook on the world marred by falsity and ignorance.

Such, or something like it, has been the fate of woman through the centuries. And if, like man, she had been light-armed for her own defence, it might have been possible to say it was her own fault that she allowed all this to take place; but when we remember that she all the while has had to bear the great and speechless burden of Sex—to be herself the ark and cradle of the Race down the ages—then we may perhaps understand what a tragedy it has all been. For the fulfillment of sex is a relief and a condensation to the Man. He goes his way, and, so to speak, thinks no more about it. But to the Woman it is the culmination of her life, her profound and secret mission to humanity, of incomparable import and delicacy.

It is difficult, of course, for men to understand the depth and sacredness of the mother-feeling in woman—its joys and hopes, its leaden weight of cares and anxieties. The burden of pregnancy and gestation, the deep inner solicitude and despondency, the fears that all may not be well, the indrawing and absorption of her life into the life of the child, the increasing effort to attend to anything else, to care for anything else; her willingness even to die if only the child may be born safe: these are things which man—except it be occasionally in his rôle as artist or inventor—does but faintly imagine. Then, later on, the dedication to the young life or lives, the years of daylong and nightlong labor and forethought, in which the very thought of self is effaced, of tender service for which there is no recognition, nor ever will or can be—except in the far future; the sacrifice of personal interests and expansions in the ever-narrowing round of domestic duty; and in the end the sad wonderment and grievous unfulfilled yearning as one by one the growing boy and girl push their way into the world and disavow their home-ties and dependence; the sundering of heartstrings even as the navel-cord had to be sundered before: for these things, too, Woman can hope but little sympathy and understanding from the other sex.

But this fact, of man's non-perception of it, does not make the tragedy less. Far back out of the brows of Greek goddess, and Sibyl, and Norse and German seeress and prophetess, over all this petty civilisation look the grand untamed eyes of a primal woman the equal and the mate of man; and in sad plight should we be if we might not already, lighting up the horizon from East and West and South and North, discern the answering looks of those newcomers who, as the period of women's enslavement is passing away, send glances of recognition across the ages to their elder sisters.

After all, and underneath all the falsities of this period, may we not say that there is a deep and permanent relation between the sexes, which must inevitably assert itself again?

To this relation the physiological differences perhaps afford the key. In woman—modern science has shown—the more fundamental and primitive nervous centres, and the great sympathetic and vaso-motor system of nerves generally, are developed to a greater extent than in man; in woman the whole structure and life rallies more closely and obviously round the sexual function than in man; and, as a general rule, in the evolution of the human race, as well as of the lower races, the female is less subject to variation and is more constant to and conservative of the type of the race than the male.* With these physiological differences are naturally allied the facts that,

* For other points of difference see "Appendix."

of the two, Woman is the more primitive, the more intuitive, the more emotional. If not so large and cosmic in her scope, the great unconscious processes of Nature lie somehow nearer to her; to her, sex is a deep and sacred instinct, carrying with it a sense of natural purity; nor does she often experience that divorce between the sentiment of Love and the physical passion which is so common with men, and which causes them to be aware of a grossness and a conflict in their own natures; she is, or should be, the interpreter of Love to man, and in some degree his guide in sexual matters. More, since she keeps to the great lines of evolution and is less biassed and influenced by the momentary currents of the day; since her life is bound up with the life of the child; since in a way she is nearer the child herself, and nearer to the savage; it is to her that Man, after his excursions and wanderings, mental and physical, continually tends to return as to his primitive home and resting-place, to restore his balance, to find his centre of life, and to draw stores of energy and inspiration for fresh conquests of the outer world. "In women men find beings who have not wandered so far as they have from the typical life of earth's creatures; women are for men the human embodiments of the restful responsiveness of Nature. To every man, as

Michelet has put it, the woman whom he loves is as the Earth was to her legendary son; he has but to fall down and kiss her breast and he is strong again."*

If it be true that by natural and physiological right Woman stands in some such primitive relationship to Man, then we may expect this relationship to emerge again into clear and reasonable light in course of time; though it does not of course follow that a relationship founded on physiological distinctions is *absolutely* permanent—since these latter may themselves vary to some degree. That a more natural and sensible relation of some kind between the sexes is actually coming to birth, few who care to read the signs of the times can well doubt. For the moment, however, and by way of parenthesis before looking to the future, we have to consider a little more in detail the present position of women under civilisation. Not that the consideration will be altogether gracious and satisfactory, but that it may—we are fain to hope—afford us some hints for the future.

It was perhaps not altogether unnatural that Man's craze for property and individual ownership should have culminated in the enslavement of

---

* *Man and Woman*, by Havelock Ellis. Contemporary Science Series, p. 371.

woman—his most precious and beloved object. But the consequence of this absurdity was a whole series of other absurdities. What between insincere flattery and rose-water adorations on the one hand, and serfdom and neglect on the other, woman was, as Havelock Ellis says, treated as "a cross between an angel and an idiot." And after a time, adapting herself to the treatment, she really became something between an angel and an idiot—a bundle of weak and flabby sentiments, combined with a wholly undeveloped brain. Moreover by being continually specialised in the sexual and domestic direction, she lost touch with the actual world, and grew, one may say, into a separate species from man—so that in the later civilisations the males and females, except when the sex-attraction has compelled them as it were to come together, have been wont to congregate in separate herds, and talk languages each unintelligible to the other. Says the author of the *Woman's Question*: "I admit there is no room for pharisaical self-laudation here. The bawling mass of *man*kind on a race-course or the stock-exchange is degrading enough in all conscience. Yet this even is hardly so painful as the sight which meets our eyes between three and four in the afternoon in any fashionable London street. Hundreds of women—mere dolls—gazing intently into shop-windows at various bits of coloured ribbon. . . . Perhaps nothing is more disheartening than this, except the mob of women in these very same streets between twelve and one at night."

The "lady," the household drudge, and the prostitute, are the three main types of woman resulting in our modern civilisation from the process of the past—and it is hard to know which is the most wretched, which is the most wronged, and which is the most unlike that which in her own heart every true woman would desire to be.

In some sense the "lady" of the period which is just beginning to pass away is the most characteristic product of Commercialism. The sense of Private Property, arising and joining with the "angel and idiot" theory, turned Woman more and more—especially of course among the possessing classes—into an emblem of possession—a mere doll, an empty idol, a brag of the man's exclusive right in the sex—till at last, as her vain splendors increased and her real usefulness diminished, she ultimated into the "perfect lady." But let every woman who piques and preens herself to the fulfillment of this ideal in her own person, remember what is the cost and what is the meaning of her quest: the covert enslavement to, and the covert contempt of Man.

The instinct of helpful personal service is so

strong in women, and such a deep-rooted part of their natures, that to be treated as a mere target for other people's worship and service—especially when this is tainted with insincerity—must be most obnoxious to them. To think that women still exist by hundreds and hundreds of thousands, women with hearts and hands formed for love and helpfulness, who are brought up as "ladies" and have to spend their lives listening to the idiotic platitudes of the Middle-class Man, and "waited upon" by wage-bought domestics, is enough to make one shudder. The modern "gentleman" is bad enough, but the "lady" of bourgeois-dom, literally "crucified twixt a smile and whimper," prostituted to a life which in her heart she hates—with its petty ideals, its narrow horizon, and its empty honors—is indeed a pitiful spectacle.

In Baronial times the household centred round the Hall, where the baron sat supreme; to-day it centres round the room where the lady reigns. The "with" is withdrawn from the withdrawing-room, and that apartment has become the most important of all. Yet there is an effect of mockery in the homage paid to the new sovereign; and, as far as her rule is actual, a doubt whether she is really qualified yet for the position. The contrast between the two societies, the Feudal and the Commercial, is not inaptly represented by this domestic change. The former society was rude and rough, but generous and straightforward; the latter is polished and nice, but full of littleness and *finesse.* The Drawing-room, with its feeble manners and effects of curtains and embroidery, gives its tone to our lives now-a-days. But we look forward to a time when this room also will cease to be the centre of the house, and another—perhaps the Common-room—will take its place.

Below a certain level in society—the distinctively commercial—there are no drawing-rooms. Among the working masses, where the woman is of indispensable importance in daily life, and is not sequestered as an idol, there is no room specially set apart for her worship—a curious change takes place in her nominal position, and whereas in the supernal sphere she sits in state and has her tea and bread and butter brought to her by obsequious males, in the cottage the men take their ease and are served by the women. The customs of the cottage, however, are rooted in a natural division of labor by which the man undertakes the outdoor, and the woman the indoor work; and there is, I think, quite as much real respect shown to her here as in the drawing-room.

In the cottage, nevertheless, the unfortunate one falls into the second pit that is prepared for her—that of the household drudge; and here she leads a life which, if it has more honesty and reality in it than that of the "lady," is one of abject slavery. Few men again realise, or trouble themselves to realise, what a life this of the working housewife is. They are accustomed to look upon their own employment, whatever it may be, as "work" (perhaps because it brings with it "wages"); the woman's they regard as a kind of pastime. They forget what monotonous drudgery it really means, and yet what incessant forethought and care; they forget that the woman has no eight hours' day, that her work is always staring her in the face, and waiting for her, even on into the night; that the body is wearied, and the mind narrowed down, "scratched to death by rats and mice" in a perpetual round of petty cares. For not only does civilisation and multifarious invention (including smoke) make the burden of domestic life immensely complex, but the point is that each housewife has to sustain this burden to herself in lonely effort. What a sight, in any of our great towns, to enter into the cottages or tenements which form the endless rows of suburban streets, and to find in each one a working wife struggling alone in semi-darkness and seclusion with the toils of an entire separate household—with meals to be planned and provided, with bread to be baked, clothes to be washed and mended, children to be kept in order, a husband to be humored, and a house to be swept and dusted; herself wearied and worried, debilitated with confinement and want of fresh air, and low-spirited for want of change and society! How futile! and how dreary!

There remains the third alternative for women; nor can it be wondered at that some deliberately choose a life of prostitution as their only escape from the existence of the lady or the drudge. Yet what a choice it is! On the one hand is the caged Woman, and on the other hand is the free: and which to choose? "How can there be a doubt," says one, "surely freedom is always best." Then there falls a hush. "Ah!" says society, pointing with its finger, "but a free *Woman!*"

And yet is it possible for Woman ever to be worthy her name, unless she is free?

To-day, or up to to-day, just as the wage-worker has had no means of livelihood except by the sale of his bodily labor, so woman has had no means of livelihood except by the surrender of her bodily sex. She could dispose of it to one man for life, and have in return the respect of society and the caged existence of the lady or the drudge, or she could sell it night by night and be a "free woman," scorned of the world and portioned to die in the gutter. In either case (if she really thinks about the matter at all) she must lose her self-respect. What a choice, what a frightful choice!—and this has been the fate of Woman for how long?

If, as a conquence of all this, woman has gone down hill, there is no doubt that man has gravitated too. (Or was it really that Jack fell down first, and "Jill came tumbling after"?) Anyhow I think that nothing can be more clear—and this I believe should be taken as the basis of any discussion on the relation of the sexes—than that whatever injures one sex injures the other; and that whatever defects or partialities may be found in the one must from the nature of the case be tallied by corresponding defects and partialities in the other. The two halves of the human race are complementary, and it is useless for one to attempt to glorify itself at the expense of the other. As in Olive Schreiner's allegory of Woman ("Three Dreams in a Desert"), man and woman are bound together by a vital band, and the one cannot move a step in advance of the other.

If we were called upon to characterise these mutual defects (inbred partly by the false property relation) we should be inclined to say they were brutality and conceit on the one hand, and *finesse* and subtlety on the other. Man, as owner, has tended to become arrogant and callous and egotistic; woman, as the owned, slavish and crafty and unreal.

As a matter of fact, and allowing that sweeping generalisations of this kind are open to a good many exceptions, we do find (at any rate in the British Isles) a most wonderful and celestial indifference to anything but their own affairs amongst the "lords of creation," an indifference so ingrained and constitutional that it is rarely conscious of itself, and which assumes quite easily and naturally that the weaker sex exists for the purpose of playing the foil, so to speak, to the chief actor in life's drama. Nor does the fact that this indifference is tempered, from time to time, by a little gallantry afford much consolation—as may be imagined—to the woman who perceives that the gallantry is inspired by nothing more than a passing sex-desire.

On the other hand Jill has come tumbling after pretty quickly, and has tumbled to the conclusion that though she cannot sway her lord by force, she may easily make use of him by craft. *Finesse,* developed through scores of generations, combined with the skilful use of the glamor belonging to her sex, have given her an extraordinary faculty of carrying out her own purposes, often through the most difficult passes, without ever exposing her hand. Possibly the knowledge of this forms one reason why women distrust each other so much more than men distrust each other. Certainly one of the rarest of God's creatures is a truly undesigning female, but—when dowered with intellect such as might seem to justify it in being designing—one of the most admirable and beautiful!

Looking a little deeper, and below the superficial contrast which an unsatisfactory relation between the sexes has doubtless created, one seems to discern some of those more vital and deep-rooted differentiations spoken of on an earlier page. It is a commonly received opinion that woman tends more to intuition and man to logic;* and certainly the male mind seems better able to deal with abstractions and generalisations, and the female mind with the personal and the detailed and the concrete. And while this difference may be in part attributable to the artificial confinement of women to the domestic sphere, there is probably something more organic in it than that. At any rate it gives to Woman some of her best qualities—a quick and immediate perception, appreciation of character, tact, and a kind of artistic sense in the ordering of her own life, so that

* Physiologically speaking a certain excess of affectability and excitability in women over men seems to be distinctly traceable.

you do not see the tags and unraveled ends which appear in man's conduct. While the man is blundering about, fighting with himself, hesitating, doubting, weighing, trying vainly to co-ordinate all the elements of his nature, the woman (often no doubt in a smaller sphere) moves serene and prompt to her ends. Her actions are characterised by grace and finality; she is more at unity with herself; and she has the inestimable advantage of living in the world of persons—which may well seem so much more important and full of interest than that of things.

On the other hand, this want of the power of generalisation has made it difficult for woman (at any rate up to to-day) to emerge from a small circle of interests, and to look at things from the point of view of public advantage and good. While her sympathies for individuals are keen and quick, abstract and general ideas such as those of Justice, Truth, and the like have been difficult of appreciation to her; and her deficiency in logic has made it almost impossible to act upon her through the brain. A man, if he is on the wrong tack, can be argued with; but with a woman of this type, if her motives are nefarious, there is no means of changing them by appeal to her reason, or to the general sense of Justice and Right—and unless controlled by the stronger sway of a determined personal will (of a man) her career is liable to be pretty bad.

Generally it will be admitted, as we are dealing with points of mental and moral difference between the sexes, Man has developed the more active, and Woman the more passive qualities; and it is pretty obvious, here too, that this difference is not only due to centuries of social inequality and of property-marriage, but roots back in some degree to the very nature of their respective sexual functions. That there are permanent complementary distinctions between the male and female, dating first perhaps from sex, and thence spreading over the whole natures, physical, mental and moral, of each, no one can reasonably doubt. These distinctions have however, we contend, been strangely accentuated and exaggerated during the historic period—till at last a point of maximum divergence and absolute misunderstanding has been reached. But that point is behind us now.

WOMAN

IN FREEDOM

IT is clear enough, from what has been said, that what Woman most needs to-day, and is mostly seeking for, is a basis of independence for her life. Nor is her position likely to be improved until she is able to face man on an equality; to find, self-balanced, her natural relation to him; and to dispose of herself and of her sex perfectly freely, and not as a thrall must do.

Doubtless if man were an ideal creature his mate might be secure of equal and considerate treatment from him without having to insist upon an absolute economic independence; but as that is only too obviously not the case there is nothing left for her to-day but to unfold the war-flag of her "rights," and (dull and tiresome as it may be) to go through a whole weary round of battles till peace is concluded again upon a better understanding.

Yet it must never be forgotten that nothing short of large social changes, stretching beyond the sphere of women only, can bring about the complete emancipation of the latter. Not till our whole commercial system, with its barter and sale of human labor and human love for gain, is done away, and not till a whole new code of ideals and customs of life has come in, will women really be free. They must remember that their cause is also the cause of the oppressed laborer over the whole earth, and the laborer has to remember that his cause is theirs.*

And since Motherhood is, after all, woman's great and incomparable work, people will come to see that a sane maternity is one of the very first things to be considered—and that really, though not the only consideration, it is a work which if properly fulfilled *does* involve the broadest and largest culture. Perhaps this might seem to some only too obvious; yet when for a moment we glance around at the current ideals, when we see what Whitman calls "the incredible holds and webs of silliness, millinery and every kind of dyspeptic depletion" in which women themselves live, when

---

* The freedom of Woman must ultimately rest on the Communism of society—which alone can give her support during the period of Motherhood, without forcing her into dependence on the arbitrary will of one man. While the present effort of women towards earning their own economic independence is a healthy sign and a necessary feature of the times, it is evident that it alone will not entirely solve the problem, since it is just during the difficult years of Motherhood, when support is most needed, that the woman is least capable of earning it for herself. (*See* "Appendix.")

we see the absolute want of training for motherhood and the increasing physical incapacity for it, and even the feminine censure of those who pass through the ordeal too easily, we begin to realise how little the present notion of what woman should be is associated with the healthy fulfillment of her most perfect work. A woman capable at all points to bear children, to guard them, to teach them, to turn them out strong and healthy citizens of the great world, stands at the farthest remove from the finnikin doll or the meek drudge whom man by a kind of false sexual selection has through many centuries evolved as his ideal.

The nervous and sexual systems of women today, ruined among the rich by a life and occupations which stimulate the emotional sensibilities without ever giving the strength and hardiness which flow from healthy and regular industry, and often ruined among the poor by excessive labor carried on under most unhealthy conditions, make real wifehood and motherhood things almost unknown. "Injudicious training," says Bebel, "miserable social conditions (food, dwelling, occupation) produce weak, bloodless, nervous beings, incapable of fulfilling the duties of matrimony. The consequences are menstrual troubles* and disturbances in the various organs connected

* *See* "Appendix."

with sexual functions, rendering maternity dangerous or impossible. Instead of a healthy, cheerful companion, a capable mother, a helpmate equal to the calls made upon her activity, the husband has a nervous excitable wife, permanently under the doctor's hands, and too fragile to bear the slightest draught or noise."

The Modern Woman sees plainly enough that no decent advance for her sex is possible until this whole question is fairly faced—involving, as of course it will do, a life very different from her present one, far more in the open air, with real bodily exercise and development, some amount of regular manual work, a knowledge of the laws of health and physiology, an altogether wider mental outlook, and greater self-reliance and nature-hardihood. But when once these things are granted, she sees that she will no longer be the serf, but the equal, the mate, and the comrade of Man.

Before any such new conception it is obvious enough that the poor little pinched ideal of the "lady," which has ruled society so long, will fade away into distance and obscurity. People may rail at the new developments, but what, it may be asked, *can* any decently sensible woman think of her present position—of the mock salutations and heroic politenesses of the conventional male—

with their suggestion of an empty homage to weakness and incapacity; of the unwritten law which condemns her, if occupying any place in society, to bridle in her chin and use an affected speech in order that it may be patent to everybody that she is *not* free; which forbids natural and spontaneous gesture as unbecoming and suspicious—and indeed in any public place as liable to the attention of the policeman; what can she think of the perpetual lies under which she has to live—too numerous to be recorded; except that all these things are intolerable? Rather than remain in such a coil the modern woman is sensible enough to see that she must face the stigma of doing things "unlady-like"; and that only by facing it can she win her true place in the world, and a real comradeship with the only class of man who is capable of such a thing—namely, the man who is willing not to be "a gentleman."

That a new code of manners between the sexes, founded not on covert lust but on open and mutual helpfulness, has got to come in, is obvious enough. The cry of equality need not like a red flag infuriate the Philistine bull. That woman is in general muscularly weaker than man, and that there are certain kinds of effort, even mental, for which she is less fitted—as there are other kinds of effort for which she is more fitted—may easily be granted; but this only means, in the language of all good manners, that there are special ways in which men can assist women, as there are special ways in which women can assist men. Anything which goes beyond this, and the friendly exchange of equal services, and which assumes, in the conventionalities of the private household or the public place, that the female claims a general indulgence (because of her general incapacity) is an offence—against the encouragement of which women themselves will no doubt be on their guard.

I say the signs of revolt on the part of the lady class—revolt long delayed but now spreading all along the line—are evident enough. When, however, we come to the second type of woman mentioned in the preceding pages, the working-wife, we—naturally enough—do not find much conscious movement. The life of the household drudge is too like that of a slave, too much consumed in mere toil, too little illuminated by any knowledge, for her to rise of herself to any other conception of existence. Nevertheless it is not difficult to see that general and social changes are working to bring about her liberation also. Improved house-construction, public bakeries and laundries, and so forth, and, what is much more important, a more rational and simple and healthful notion of food and furniture, are tending very largely to reduce the labors of housework and cookery; and conservative though women are in their habits, when these changes are brought to their doors they cannot but see the advantage of them. Public institutions too are more and more taking over the responsibilities and the cost of educating and rearing children; and even here and there we may discern a drift towards the amalgamation of households, which by introducing a common life and division of labor among the women-folk will probably do much to cheer and lighten their lot. None of these changes, however, will be of great use unless or until they wake the overworked woman herself to see and insist on her rights to a better life, and until they force from the man a frank acknowledgment of her claim. And surely here and there the man himself will do something to educate his mate to this point. We see no reason indeed why he should not assist in some part of the domestic work, and thus contribute his share of labor and intelligence to the conduct of the house; nor why the woman—being thus relieved—should not occasionally, and when desirable, find salaried work outside, and so contribute to the maintenance of the family, and to her own security and sense of independence. The over-differentiation of the labors of the sexes to-day is at once a perpetuation of the servitude of women and a cause of misunderstanding between her and man, and of lack of interest in each other's doings.

The third type of woman, the prostitute, provides us with that question which—according to Bebel—is the sphinx-riddle that modern society cannot solve, and yet which unsolved threatens society's destruction. The commercial prostitution of love is the last outcome of our whole social system, and its most clear condemnation. It flaunts in our streets, it hides itself in the garment of respectability under the name of matrimony, it eats in actual physical disease and death right through our midst; it is fed by the oppression and the ignorance of women, by their poverty and denied means of livelihood, and by the hypocritical puritanism which forbids them by millions not only to gratify but even to speak of their natural desires; and it is encouraged by the callousness of an age which has accustomed men to buy and sell for money every most precious thing—even the life-long labor of their brothers, therefore why not also the very bodies of their sisters?

Here there is no solution *except* the freedom of woman—which means of course also the freedom of the masses of the people, men and women, and the ceasing altogether of economic slavery.

There is no solution which will not include the redemption of the terms "free woman" and "free love" to their *true* and rightful significance. Let every woman whose heart bleeds for the sufferings of her sex, hasten to declare herself and to constitute herself, as far as she possibly can, a free woman. Let her accept the term with all the odium that belongs to it; let her insist on her right to speak, dress, think, act, and above all to use her sex, as she deems best; let her face the scorn and ridicule; let her "lose her own life" if she likes; assured that only so can come deliverance, and that only when the free woman is honored will the prostitute cease to exist. And let every man who really would respect his counterpart, entreat her also to act so; let him never by word or deed tempt her to grant as a bargain what can only be precious as a gift; let him see her with pleasure stand a little aloof; let him help her to gain her feet; so at last, by what slight sacrifices on his part such a course may involve, will it dawn upon him that he has gained a real companion and helpmate on life's journey.

The whole evil of commercial prostitution arises out of the domination of Man in matters of sex. Better indeed were a Saturnalia of *free* men and women than the spectacle which as it is our great cities present at night. Here in Sex, the women's instincts are, as a rule, so clean, so direct, so well-rooted in the needs of the race, that except for man's domination they would scarcely have suffered this perversion. Sex in man is an unorganised passion, an individual need or impetus; but in woman it may more properly be termed a constructive instinct, with the larger signification that that involves. Even more than man should woman be "free" to work out the problem of her sex-relations as may commend itself best to her—hampered as little as possible by legal, conventional, or economic considerations, and relying chiefly on her own native sense and tact in the matter. Once thus free—free from the mere cash-nexus to a husband, from the money-slavery of the streets, from the nameless terrors of social opinion, and from the threats of the choice of perpetual virginity or perpetual bondage—would she not indeed choose her career (whether that of wife and mother, or that of free companion, or one of single blessedness) far better for herself than it is chosen *for* her to-day—regarding really in some degree the needs of society, and the welfare of children, and the sincerity and durability of her relations to her lovers, and less the petty motives of profit and fear?

The point is that the whole conception of a nobler Womanhood for the future has to proceed candidly from this basis of her complete freedom as to the disposal of her sex, and from the healthy conviction that, with whatever individual aberrations, she will on the whole use that freedom rationally and well. And surely this—in view too of some decent education of the young on sexual matters—is not too great a demand to make on our faith in women. If it is, then indeed we are undone—for short of this we can only retain them in servitude, and society in its form of the hell on earth which it largely is to-day.

Refreshing therefore in its way is the spirit of revolt which is spreading on all sides. Let us hope such revolt will continue. If it lead here and there to strained or false situations, or to temporary misunderstandings—still, declared enmity is better than unreal acquiescence. Too long have women acted the part of mere appendages to the male, suppressing their own individuality and fostering his self-conceit. In order to have souls of their own they must free themselves, and greatly by their own efforts. They must learn to fight. Whitman in his poem "A woman waits for me," draws a picture of a woman who stands in the sharpest possible contrast with the feeble bourgeois ideal—a woman who can "swim, row, ride, wrestle, shoot, run, strike, retreat, defend herself," etc.; and Bebel, in his book on Woman, while pointing out that in Sparta, "where the greatest attention was paid to the physical development of both sexes, boys and girls went about naked till they had reached the age of puberty, and were trained together in bodily exercises, games and wrestling," complains that nowadays "the notion that women require strength, courage and resolution is regarded as very heterodox." But the truth is that qualities of courage and independence are not agreeable in a slave, and that is why man during all these centuries has consistently discountenanced them—till at last the female herself has come to consider them "unwomanly." Yet this last epithet is absurd; for if tenderness is the crown and glory of woman, nothing can be more certain than that true tenderness is only found in strong and courageous natures; the tenderness of a servile person is no tenderness at all.

It has not escaped the attention of thinkers on these subjects that the rise of Women into freedom and larger social life here alluded to—and already indeed indicated by the march of events—is likely to have a profound influence on the future of our race. It is pointed out that among most of the higher animals, and indeed among many of the early races of mankind, the males have been selected by the females on account of their prowess or superior strength or beauty, and this has led to the evolution in the males and in the race at large of a type which (in a dim and unconscious manner) was the ideal of the female.* But as soon as in the history of mankind the property-love set in, and woman became the chattel of man, this action ceased. She, being no longer free, could not possibly choose man, but rather the opposite took place, and man began to select woman for the characteristics pleasing to *him*. The latter now adorned herself to gratify his taste, and the female type and consequently the type of the whole race have been correspondingly affected. With the return of woman to freedom the ideal of the female may again resume its sway. It is possible indeed that the more dignified and serious attitude of women towards sex may give to sexual selection when exercised by them a nobler influence than when exercised by the males. Anyhow it is not difficult to see that women really free would never countenance for their mates the many mean and unclean types of men who to-day seem to have things all their own way, nor consent to have children by such men; nor is it difficult to imagine that the feminine influence might thus sway to the evolution of a more manly and dignified race

* *See* "Appendix."

than has been disclosed in these last days of commercial civilisation!

The Modern Woman with her clubs, her debates, her politics, her freedom of action and costume, is forming a public opinion of her own at an amazing rate; and seems to be preparing to "spank" and even thump the Middle-class Man in real earnest! What exactly evolution may be preparing for us, we do not know, but apparently some lively sparring matches between the sexes. Of course all will not be smooth sailing. The women of the new movement are naturally largely drawn from those in whom the maternal instinct is not especially strong; also from those in whom the sexual instinct is not preponderant. Such women do not altogether represent their sex; some are rather mannish in temperament; some are "homogenic," that is, inclined to attachments to their own, rather than to the opposite, sex; some are ultra-rationalizing and brain-cultured; to many, children are more or less a bore; to others, man's sex-passion is a mere impertinence, which they do not understand, and whose place they consequently misjudge. It would not do to say that the majority of the new movement are thus out of line, but there is no doubt that a large number are, and the course of their progress will be correspondingly curvilinear.

Perhaps the deficiency in maternal instinct would seem the most serious imputation. But then, who knows (as we have said) what evolution is preparing? Sometimes it seems possible that a new sex is on the make—like the feminine neuters of Ants and Bees—not adapted for child-bearing, but with a marvelous and perfect instinct of social service, indispensable for the maintenance of the common life. Certainly most of those who are freeing themselves—often with serious struggles—from the "lady" chrysalis are fired with an ardent social enthusiasm; and if they may personally differ in some respects from the average of their sex, it is certain that their efforts will result in a tremendous improvement in the general position of their more commonplace sisters.

If it should turn out that a certain fraction of the feminine sex should for one reason or another not devote itself to the work of maternity, still the influence of this section would react on the others to render their notion of motherhood far more dignified than before. There is not much doubt that in the future this most important of human labors will be carried on with a degree of conscious intelligence hitherto unknown, and which will raise it from the fulfillment of a mere instinct to the completion of a splendid social purpose. To save the souls of children as well as their bodies, to raise heroic as well as prosperous citizens, will surely be the desire and the work of the mothers of our race.*

It will perhaps be said that after going about to show (as in the previous chapter) the deficiency of women hitherto in the matter of the generalising faculty, it is somewhat inconsistent to express any great hope that they will ever take much active interest in the general social life to which they belong; but indeed the answer to this is that they are already beginning to do so. The social enthusiasm and activity shown by women in Britain, Russia, and the United States is so great and well-rooted that it is impossible to believe it a mere ephemeral event; and though in the older of these countries it is at present confined to the more wealthy classes, we can augur from that—according to a well-known principle—that it will in time spread downwards to the women of the nation.

Important as is the tendency of women in the countries mentioned to higher education and brain

* As to the maternal teaching of children, it must be confessed that it has, in late times, been most dismal. Whether among the masses or the classes the idea has been first and foremost to impress upon them the necessity of sliding through life as comfortably as possible, and the parting word to the boy leaving home to launch into the great world has seldom risen to a more heroic strain than "Don't forget your flannels!"

development, I think it is evident that the widening and socialisation of their interests is not taking place so much through mere study of books and the passing of examinations in political economy and other sciences, as through the extended actual experience which the life of the day is bringing to them. Certainly the book-studies are important and must not be neglected; but above all is it imperative (and men, if they are to have any direct sway in the future destinies of the other sex, must look to it) that women, so long confined to the narrowest mere routine and limited circle of domestic life, should see and get experience, all they can, of the actual world. The theory, happily now exploding, of keeping them "innocent" through sheer ignorance partakes too much of the "angel and idiot" view. To see the life of slum and palace and workshop, to enter into the trades and professions, to become doctors, nurses, and so forth, to have to look after themselves and to hold their own as against men, to travel, to meet with sexual experience, to work together in trade-unions, to join in social and political uprisings and rebellions, etc., is what women want just now. And it is evident enough that at any rate among the more prosperous sections in this country such a movement is going on apace. If the existence of the enormous hordes of unattached females that we find living on interest and dividends to-day is a blemish from a Socialistic point of view; if we find them on the prowl all over the country, filling the theatres and concert-rooms and public entertainments in the proportion of three to one male, besetting the trains, swarming onto the tops of the 'buses, dodging on bicycles under the horses' heads, making speeches at street corners, blocking the very pavements in front of fashionable shops, we must not forget that for the objects we have just sketched, even this class is going the most direct way to work, and laying in stores of experience, which will make it impossible for it ever to return to the petty life of times gone by.

At the last, and after centuries of misunderstanding and association of triviality and superficiality with the female sex, it will perhaps dawn upon the world that the truth really lies in an opposite direction—that, in a sense, there is something more deep-lying, fundamental and primitive in the woman nature than in that of the man; that instead of being the over-sensitive hysterical creature that civilisation has too often made her, she is essentially of calm large and acceptive even though emotional temperament. "Her shape arises," says Walt Whitman,

> "She less guarded than ever, yet more guarded than ever,
> The gross and soil'd she moves among do not make her gross and soil'd,
> She knows the thoughts as she passes, nothing is concealed from her,
> She is none the less considerate or friendly therefor,
> She is the best belov'd, it is without exception; she has no reason to fear, and she does not fear."

The Greek goddesses look down and across the ages to the very outposts beyond civilisation; and already from America, Australasia, Africa, Norway, Russia, as even in our midst from those who have crossed the border-line of all class and caste, glance forth the features of a grander type—fearless and untamed—the primal merging into the future Woman; who, combining broad sense with sensibility, the passion for Nature with the love of Man, and commanding indeed the details of life, yet risen out of localism and convention, will help us to undo the bands of death which encircle the present society, and open the doors to a new and a wider life.

MARRIAGE

A RETROSPECT

OF the great mystery of human Love, and that most intimate personal relation of two souls to each other—perhaps the firmest, most basic and indissoluble fact (after our own existence) that we know; of that strange sense—often, perhaps generally, instantaneous—of long precedent familiarity and kinship, that deep reliance on and acceptation of another in his or her entirety; of the tremendous strength of the chain which thus at times will bind two hearts in lifelong dedication and devotion, persuading and indeed not seldom compelling the persons concerned to the sacrifice of some of the other elements of their lives and characters; and, withal, of a certain inscrutable veiledness from each other which so frequently accompanies the relation of the opposite sexes, and which forms at once the abiding charm, and the pain, sometimes the tragedy, of their union; of this palpitating winged living thing, which one may perhaps call the real Marriage—I would say but little; for indeed it is only fitting or possible to speak of it by indirect language and suggestion, nor may one venture to drag it rudely from its sanctuary into the light of the common gaze.

Compared with this, the actual marriage, in its squalid perversity as we too often have occasion of knowing it, is as the wretched idol of the savage to the reality which it is supposed to represent; and one seems to hear the Aristophanic laughter of the gods as they contemplate man's little clay image of the Heavenly Love—which, cracked in the fire of daily life, he is fain to bind together with rusty hoops of law, and parchment bonds, lest it should crumble and fall to pieces altogether.

The whole subject, wide as life itself—as Heaven and Hell—eludes anything like adequate treatment, and we need make no apology for narrowing down our considerations here to just a few practical points; and if we cannot navigate upward into the very heart of the matter—namely, into the causes which make some people love each other with a true and perfect love, and others unite in obedience to but a counterfeit passion—yet we may fairly, I imagine, study some of the conditions which give to actual marriage its present form, or which in the future are likely to provide real affection with a more satisfactory expression than it has as a rule to-day.

As long as man is only half-grown, and woman is a serf or a parasite, it can hardly be expected that Marriage should be particularly successful. Two people come together, who know but little of each other, who have been brought up along different lines, who certainly do not understand each other's nature; whose mental interests and occupations are different, whose worldly interests and advantage are also different; to one of whom the subject of sex is probably a sealed book, to the other perhaps a book whose most dismal page has been opened first. The man needs an outlet for his passion; the girl is looking for a "home" and a proprietor. A glamor of illusion descends upon the two, and drives them into each other's arms. It envelops in a gracious and misty halo all their differences and misapprehensions. They marry without misgiving; and their hearts overflow with gratitude to the white-surpliced old gentleman who reads the service over them.

But at a later hour, and with calmer thought, they begin to realise that it is a life-sentence which he has so suavely passed upon them—not reducible (as in the case of ordinary convicts) even to a term of 20 years. The brief burst of their first satisfaction has been followed by a satiety on the physical plane, then by mere vacuity of affection, then by boredom, and even nausea. The girl, full perhaps of a tender emotion, and missing the sympathy and consolation she expected in the man's love, only to find its more materialistic side—"This, this then is what I am wanted for"; the man, who looked for a companion, finding he can rouse no mortal interest in his wife's mind save in the most exasperating trivialities;—whatever the cause may be, a veil has fallen from before their faces, and there they sit, held together now by the least honorable interests, the interests which they themselves can least respect, but to which Law and Religion lend all their weight. The monetary dependence of the woman, the mere sex-needs of the man, the fear of public opinion, all form motives, and motives of the meanest kind, for maintaining the seeming tie; and the relation of the two hardens down into a dull neutrality, in which lives and characters are narrowed and blunted, and deceit becomes the common weapon which guards divided interests.

A sad picture! and of course in this case a portrayal deliberately of the seamy side of the matter. But who shall say what agonies are often gone through in those first few years of married life? Anyhow, this is the sort of problem which we have to face to-day, and which shows its actuality by the amazing rate at which it is breaking out in literature on all sides.

It may be said—and often of course is said—that such cases as these only prove that marriage was entered into under the influence of a passing glamor and delusion, and that there was not much real devotion to begin with. And no doubt there is truth enough in such remarks. But—we may say in reply—because two people make a mistake in youth, to condemn them, for that reason, to lifelong suffering and mutual degradation, or to see them so condemned, without proposing any hope or way of deliverance, but with the one word "serves you right" on the lips, is a course which can commend itself only to the grimmest and dullest Calvinist. Whatever safe-guards against a too frivolous view of the relationship may be proposed by the good sense of society in the future, it is certain that the time has gone past when Marriage can continue to be regarded as a supernatural institution to whose maintenance human bodies and souls must be indiscriminately sacrificed; a humaner, wiser, and less panic-stricken treatment of the subject must set in; and if there are difficulties in the way they must be met by patient and calm consideration of human welfare—superior to any law, however ancient and respectable.

I take it then that, without disguising the fact that the question is a complex one, and that our conclusions may be only very tentative, we have to consider as rationally as we conveniently can, first, some of the drawbacks or defects of the present marriage customs, and secondly such improvements in these as may seem feasible.

And with regard to the former, one of the most important points—which we have already touched on—is the extraordinary absence of any allusion to these subjects in the teaching of young folk. In a day when every possible study seems to be crammed into the school curriculum, it is curious that the one matter which is of supreme importance to the individual and the community is most carefully ignored. That one ought to be able to distinguish a passing sex-spell from a true comradeship and devotion is no doubt a very sapient remark; but since it is a thing which mature folk often fail to do, how young things with no experience of their own or hint from others should be expected to do it is not easy to understand. The search for a fitting mate, especially among the more sensitive and highly-organised types of mankind, is a very complex affair; and it is really monstrous that the girl or youth should have to set out—as they mostly have to do to-day—on this difficult quest without a word of help as to the choice of the way or the very real doubts and perplexities that beset it.

If the pair whom we have supposed as about to be married had been brought up in almost any tribe of savages, they would a few years previously have gone through regular offices of initiation into manhood and womanhood, during which time ceremonies (possibly indecent in our eyes) would at any rate have made many misapprehensions impossible. As it is, the civilised girl is led to the "altar" often in uttermost ignorance and misunderstanding as to the nature of the sacrificial rites about to be consummated. The youth too is ignorant in his way. Perhaps he is unaware that love in the female is, in a sense, more diffused than in the male, less specially sexual: that it dwells longer in caresses and embraces, and determines itself more slowly towards the reproductive system. Impatient, he injures and horrifies his partner, and unconsciously perhaps aggravates the very hysterical tendency which marriage might and should have allayed.*

Among the middle and well-to-do classes especially the conditions of high civilisation, by induc-

* It must be remembered too that to many women (though of course by no means a majority) the thought of Sex brings but little sense of pleasure, and the fulfillment of its duties constitutes a real, even though a willing, sacrifice. *See* "Appendix."

ing an overfed masculinity in the males and a nervous and hysterical tendency in the females,* increase the difficulties mentioned; and it is among the "classes" too that the special evils exist of sex-starvation and sex-ignorance on the one hand, and of mere licentiousness on the other.

Among the comparatively uncivilised mass of the people, where a good deal of familiarity between the sexes takes place before marriage, and where probably there is less ignorance on the one side and less licentiousness on the other, these ills are not so prominent. But here too the need for some sensible teaching is clear; and sheer neglect of the law of Transmutation, or sheer want of self-control, are liable to make the proletarian union brutish enough.

So far with regard to difficulties arising from personal ignorance and inexperience. But stretching beyond and around all these are those others that arise from the special property-relation between the two sexes, and from deep-lying historic and economic causes generally. The long historic serfdom of woman, creeping down into the moral

* Thus Bebel in his book on *Woman* speaks of "the idle and luxurious life of so many women in the upper classes, the nervous stimulant afforded by exquisite perfumes, the over-dosing with poetry, music, the stage—which is regarded as the chief means of education, and is the chief occupation, of a sex already suffering from hypertrophy of nerves and sensibility."

and intellectual natures of the two sexes, has exaggerated the naturally complementary relation of the male and the female into an absurd caricature of strength on the one hand and dependence on the other. This is well seen in the ordinary marriage-relation of the common-prayer-book type. The frail and delicate female is supposed to cling round the sturdy husband's form, or to depend from his arm in graceful incapacity; and the spectator is called upon to admire the charming effect of the union—as of the ivy with the oak—forgetful of the terrible moral, namely, that (in the case of the trees at any rate) it is really a death-struggle which is going on, in which either the oak must perish suffocated in the embraces of its partner, or in order to free the former into anything like healthy development the ivy must be sacrificed.

Too often of course of such marriages the egoism, lordship and physical satisfaction of the man are the chief motive causes. The woman is practically sacrificed to the part of the maintenance of these male virtues. It is for her to spend her days in little forgotten details of labor and anxiety for the sake of the man's superior comfort and importance, to give up her needs to his whims, to "humor" him in all ways she can; it is for her to wipe her mind clear of all opinions in order that she may hold it up as a kind of mirror in which he may behold reflected his lordly self; and it is for her to sacrifice even her physical health and natural instincts in deference to what is called her "duty" to her husband.

How bitterly *alone* many such a woman feels! She has dreamed of being folded in the arms of a strong man, and surrendering herself, her life, her mind, her all, to his service. Of course it is an unhealthy dream, an illusion, a mere luxury of love; and it is destined to be dashed. She has to learn that self-surrender may be just as great a crime as self-assertion. She finds that her very willingness to be sacrificed only fosters in the man, perhaps for his own self-defence, the egotism and coldness that so cruelly wound her.

For how often does he with keen prevision see that if he gives way from his coldness the clinging dependent creature will infallibly overgrow and smother him!—that she will cut her woman-friends, will throw aside all her own interests and pursuits in order to "devote" herself to him, and, affording no sturdy character of her own in which *he* can take any interest, will hang the festoons of her affection on every ramification of his wretched life—nor leave him a corner free—till he perishes from all manhood and social or heroic uses into a mere matrimonial clothespeg, a warning and a wonderment to passers by!

However, as an alternative, it sometimes happens that the Woman, too wise to sacrifice her own life indiscriminately to the egoism of her husband, and not caring for the "festoon" method, adopts the middle course of *appearing* to minister to him while really pursuing her own purposes. She cultivates the gentle science of indirectness. While holding up a mirror for the Man to admire himself in, *behind that mirror* she goes her own way and carries out her own designs separate from him; and while sacrificing her body to his wants, she does so quite deliberately and for a definite reason, namely, because she has found out that she can so get a shelter for herself and her children, and can solve the problem of that maintenance which society has hitherto denied to her in her own right. For indeed by a cruel fate women have been placed in exactly that position where the sacrifice of their self-respect for base motives has easily passed beyond a temptation into being a necessity. They have had to live, and have too often only been able to do so by selling themselves into bondage to the man. Willing or unwilling, overworked or dying, they have had to bear children to the caprice of their lords; and in this serf-life their very natures have been blunted; they have lost—what indeed should be the very glory and crown of woman's being—the perfect freedom and the purity of their love.*

At this whole spectacle of woman's degradation the human male has looked on with stupid and open-mouthed indifference—as an ox might look on at a drowning ox-herd—not even dimly divining that his own fate was somehow involved. He has calmly and obliviously watched the woman drift farther and farther away from him, till at last, with the loss of an intelligent and mutual understanding between the sexes, Love with unequal wings has fallen lamed to the ground. Yet it would be idle to deny that even in such a state of affairs as that depicted, men and women have in the past and do often even now find some degree of satisfaction—simply indeed because their types of character are such as belong to, and have been evolved in accordance with, this relation.

To-day, however, there are thousands of women—and every day more thousands—to whom such a lopsided alliance is detestable; who are determined that they will no longer endure the arrogant lordship and egoism of men, nor countenance in themselves or other women the craft and servility which are the necessary complements of the relation; who see too clearly in

---

* *See* "Appendix."

the oak-and-ivy marriage its parasitism on the one hand and strangulation on the other to be sensible of any picturesqueness; who feel too that they have capacities and powers of their own which need space and liberty, and some degree of sympathy and help, for their unfolding; and who believe that they have work to do in the world, as important in its own way as any that men do in theirs. Such women have broken into open warfare—not against marriage, but against a marriage which makes true and equal love an impossibility. They feel that as long as women are economically dependent they *cannot* stand up for themselves and insist on those rights which men from stupidity and selfishness will not voluntarily grant them.

On the other hand there are thousands—and one would hope every day more thousands—of men who (whatever their forerunners may have thought) do *not* desire or think it delightful to have a glass continually held up for them to admire themselves in; who look for a partner in whose life and pursuits they can find some interest, rather than for one who has no interest but in them; who think perhaps that they would rather minister than be (like a monkey fed with nuts in a cage) the melancholy object of another person's ministrations; and who at any rate feel that love, in order to be love at all, must be absolutely open and sincere, and free from any sentiment of dependence or inequality. They see that the present cramped condition of women is not only the cause of the false relation between the sexes, but that it is the fruitful source—through its debarment of any common interests—of that fatal boredom of which we have spoken, and which is the bugbear of marriage; and they would gladly surrender all of that masterhood and authority which is supposed to be their due, if they could only get in return something like a frank and level comradeship.

Thus while we see in the present inequality of the sexes an undoubted source of marriage troubles and unsatisfactory alliances, we see also forces at work which are tending to reaction, and to bringing the two nearer again to each other—so that while differentiated they will not perhaps in the future be quite so *much* differentiated as now, but only to a degree which will enhance and adorn, instead of destroy, their sense of mutual sympathy.

There is another point which ought to be considered as contributing to the ill-success of many marriages, and which no doubt is closely connected with that just discussed—but which deserves separate treatment. I mean the harshness of the line, the kind of "ring-fence," which social opinion (at any rate in this country) draws round the married pair with respect to their relations to outsiders. On the one hand, and within the fence, society allows practically the utmost passional excess or indulgence, and condones it; on the other hand (I am speaking of the middling bulk of the people, not of the extreme aristocratic and slum classes) beyond that limit, the slightest familiarity or any expression of affection which might by any possibility be interpreted as deriving from sexual feeling, is sternly anathematised. Marriage, by a kind of absurd fiction, is represented as an oasis situated in the midst of an arid desert—in which latter, it is pretended, neither of the two parties is so fortunate as to find any objects of real affectional interest. If they do they have carefully to conceal the same from the other party.

The result of this convention is obvious enough. The married pair, thus *driven* as well as drawn into closest continual contact with each other, are put through an ordeal which might well cause the stoutest affection to quail. To have to spend all your life with another person is severe; but to have all outside personal interests, except of the most abstract kind, debarred, and if there happens to be any natural jealousy in the case, to have it tenfold increased by public interference, is terrible; and yet unless the contracting parties are fortunate enough to be, both of them, of such a temperament that they are capable of strong attachments to persons of their own sex—and this does not always exclude jealousy—such must be their fate.

It is hardly necessary to say, not only how dull a place this makes the home, but also how narrowing it acts on the lives of the married pair. However appropriate the union may be in itself it cannot be good that it should degenerate—as it tends to degenerate so often, and where man and wife are most faithful to each other—into a mere *égoisme à deux*. And right enough no doubt as a great number of such unions actually are, it must be confessed that the bourgeois marriage as a rule, and just in its most successful and pious and respectable form, carries with it an odious sense of stuffiness and narrowness, moral and intellectual; and that the type of Family which it provides is too often like that which is disclosed when on turning over a large stone we disturb an insect home that seldom sees the light.

But in cases where the marriage does not happen to be particularly successful or unsuccessful, when perhaps a true but not overpoweringly intense affection is satiated at a needlessly early stage by the continual and unrelieved impingement of the two personalities on each other, then the boredom resulting is something frightful to contemplate—and all the more so because of the genuine affection behind it, which contemplates with horror its own suicide. The weary couples that may be seen at seaside places and pleasure resorts—the respectable working-man with his wife trailing along by his side, or the highly respectable stock-jobber arm-in-arm with his better and larger half—their blank faces, utter want of any common topic of conversation which has not been exhausted a thousand times already, and their obvious relief when the hour comes which will take them back to their several and divided occupations—these illustrate sufficiently what I mean. The curious thing is that jealousy (accentuated as it is by social opinion) sometimes increases in exact proportion to mutual boredom; and there are thousands of cases of married couples leading a cat-and-dog life, and knowing that they weary each other to distraction, who for that very reason dread all the more to lose sight of each other, and thus never get a chance of that holiday from their own society, and renewal of outside interests, which would make a real good time for them possible.

Thus the sharpness of the line which society draws around the pair, and the kind of fatal snapof-the-lock with which marriage suddenly cuts them off from the world, not only precluding the two, as might fairly be thought advisable, from sexual, but also barring any openly affectional relations with outsiders, and corroborating the selfish sense of monopoly which each has in the other—these things lead inevitably to the narrowing down of lives and the blunting of general human interests, to intense mutual ennui, and when (as an escape from these evils) outside relations are covertly indulged in, to prolonged and systematic deceit.

From all which the only conclusion seems to be that marriage must be either alive or dead. As a dead thing it can of course be petrified into a hard and fast formula, but if it is to be a living bond, that living bond must be trusted to, to hold the lovers together; nor be too forcibly stiffened and contracted by private jealousy and public censorship, lest the thing that it would preserve for us perish so, and cease altogether to be beautiful. It is the same with this as with anything else. If we would have a living thing, we must give that thing some degree of liberty—even though liberty bring with it risk. If we would debar all liberty and all risk, then we can have only the mummy and dead husk of the thing.

Thus far I have had the somewhat invidious

task, but perhaps necessary as a preliminary one, of dwelling on the defects and drawbacks of the present marriage system. I am sensible that, with due discretion, some things might have been said, which have not been said, in its praise; its successful, instead of its unsuccessful, instances might have been cited; and taking for granted the dependence of women, and other points which have already been sufficiently discussed, it might have been possible to show that the bourgeois arrangement was on the whole as satisfactory as could be expected. But such a course would neither have been sincere nor have served any practical purpose. In view of the actually changing relations between the sexes, it is obvious that changes in the form of the marriage institution are impending, and the questions which are really pressing on folks' mind are: What are those changes going to be? and, Of what kind do we wish them to be?

MARRIAGE

A FORECAST

IN answer to the last question it is not improbable that the casual reader might suppose the writer of these pages to be in favor of a general loosening of all ties—for indeed it is always easy to draw a large inference even from the simplest expression.

But such a conclusion would be rash. There is little doubt, I think, that the compulsion of the marriage-tie (whether moral, social, or merely legal) acts beneficially in a considerable number of cases—though it is obvious that the more the compelling force takes a moral or social form and the less purely legal it is, the better; and that any changes which led to a cheap and continual transfer of affections from one object to another would be disastrous both to the character and happiness of a population. While we cannot help seeing that the marriage-relation—in order to become the indwelling-place of Love—must be made far more *free* than it is at present, we may also recognise that a certain amount of external pressure is not (as things are at least) without its uses: that, for instance, it tends on the whole to concentrate affectional experience and romance on one object, and that though this may mean a loss at times in breadth it means a gain in depth and intensity; that, in many cases, if it were not for some kind of bond, the two parties, after their first passion for each other was past, and when the unavoidable period of friction had set in, might in a moment of irritation easily fly apart, whereas being forced for a while to tolerate each other's defects they learn thereby one of the best lessons of life—a tender forbearance and gentleness, which as time goes on does not unfrequently deepen again into a more pure and perfect love even than at first—a love founded indeed on the first physical intimacy, but concentrated and intensified by years of linked experience, of twined associations, of shared labors, and of mutual forgiveness; and in the third place that the existence of a distinct tie or pledge discredits the easily-current idea that mere pleasure-seeking is to be the object of the association of the sexes—a phantasmal and delusive notion, which if it once got its head, and the bit between its teeth, might soon dash the car of human advance in ruin to the ground.

But having said thus much, it is obvious that external public opinion and pressure are looked upon only as having an *educational* value; and the question arises whether there is beneath this any *reality* of marriage which will ultimately emerge and make itself felt, enabling men and women to order their relations to each other, and to walk freely, unhampered by props or pressures from without.

And it would hardly be worth while writing on this subject, if one did not believe in some such reality. Practically I do not doubt that the more people think about these matters, and the more experience they have, the more they must ever come to feel that there *is* such a thing as a permanent and life-long union—perhaps a many-life-long union—founded on some deep elements of attachment and congruity in character; and the more they must come to prize the constancy and loyalty which rivets such unions, in comparison with the fickle passion which tends to dissipate them.

In all men who have reached a certain grade of evolution, and certainly in almost all women, the deep rousing of the sexual nature carries with it a romance and tender emotional yearning towards the object of affection, which lasts on and is not forgotten, even when the sexual attraction has ceased to be strongly felt. This, in favorable cases, forms the basis of what may almost be called an amalgamated personality. That there should exist one other person in the world towards whom all openness of interchange should establish itself, from whom there should be no concealment; whose body should be as dear to one, in every part, as one's own; with whom there should be no sense of Mine or Thine, in property or possession; into whose mind one's thoughts should naturally flow, as it were to know themselves and to receive a new illumination; and between whom and oneself there should be a spontaneous rebound of sympathy in all the joys and sorrows and experiences of life; such is perhaps one of the dearest wishes of the soul. It is obvious, however, that this state of affairs cannot be reached at a single leap, but must be the gradual result of years of intertwined memory and affection. For such a union Love must lay the foundation, but patience and gentle consideration and self-control must work unremittingly to perfect the structure. At length each lover comes to know the complexion of the other's mind, the wants, bodily and mental, the needs, the regrets, the satisfactions of the other, almost as his or her own—and without prejudice in favor of self rather than in favor of the other; above all, both parties come to know in course of time, and after perhaps some doubts and trials, that the great want, the great need, which holds them together, is not going to fade away into thin air; but is going to become stronger and more indefeasible as the years go on. There falls a sweet, an irresistible, trust over their relation to each other, which consecrates as it were the double life, making both feel that nothing can now divide; and robbing each of all desire to remain, when death has indeed (or at least in outer semblance) removed the other.*

So perfect and gracious a union—even if not always realised—is still, I say, the *bona fide* desire of most of those who have ever thought about such matters. It obviously yields far more and more enduring joy and satisfaction in life than any number of frivolous relationships. It commends itself to the common sense, so to speak, of the modern mind—and does not require, for its proof, the artificial authority of Church and State. At the same time it is equally evident—and a child could understand this—that it requires some rational forbearance and self-control for its realisation, and it is quite intelligible too, as already said, that there *may* be cases in which a little outside pressure, of social opinion, or even actual law may be helpful for the sup-

* It is curious that the early Church Service had "Till death us depart," but in 1661 this was altered to "Till death us do part."

plementing or reinforcement of the weak personal self-control of those concerned.

The modern Monogamic Marriage however, certified and sanctioned by Church and State, though apparently directed to this ideal, has for the most part fallen short of it. For in constituting—as in a vast number of cases—a union resting on *nothing* but the outside pressure of Church and State, it constituted a thing obviously and by its nature bad and degrading; while in its more successful instances by a too great exclusiveness it has condemned itself to a fatal narrowness and stuffiness.

Looking back to the historical and physiological aspects of the question it might of course be contended—and probably with some truth—that the human male is, by his nature and needs, polygamous. Nor is it necessary to suppose that polygamy in certain countries and races is by any means so degrading or unsuccessful an institution as some folk would have it to be.* But, as Letourneau in his "Evolution of Marriage" points out, the progress of society in the past has on the whole been from confusion to dis-

* See R. F. Burton's *Pilgrimage to El-Medinah and Meccah*, chap. xxiv. He says however, "As far as my limited observations go *polyandry* is the only state of society in which jealousy and quarrels about the sex are the exception and not the rule of life!"

tinction; and we may fairly suppose that with the progress of our own race (for each race no doubt has its special genius in such matters), and as the spiritual and emotional sides of man develop in relation to the physical, there is probably a tendency for our deeper alliances to become more unitary. Though it might be said that the growing complexity of man's nature would be likely to lead him into more rather than fewer relationships, yet on the other hand it is obvious that as the depth and subtlety of any attachment that will really hold him increases, so does such attachment become more permanent and durable, and less likely to be realised in a number of persons. Woman, on the other hand, cannot be said to be by her physical nature polyandrous as man is polygynous. Though of course there are plenty of examples of women living in a state of polyandry both among savage and civilised peoples, yet her more limited sexual needs, and her long periods of gestation, render one mate physically sufficient for her; while her more clinging affectional nature perhaps accentuates her capacity of absorption in the one.

In both man and woman then we may say that we find a distinct tendency towards the formation of this double unit of wedded life (I hardly like to use the word Monogamy on account of its sad associations)—and while we do not want to stamp such natural unions with any false irrevocability or dogmatic exclusiveness, what we do want is a recognition to-day of the tendency to their formation as a natural *fact*, independent of any artificial laws, just as one might believe in the natural bias of two atoms of certain different chemical substances to form a permanent compound atom or molecule.

It might not be so very difficult to get quite young people to understand this—to understand that even though they may have to contend with some superfluity of passion in early years, yet that the most deep-rooted desire within them will probably in the end point to a permanent union with one mate; and that towards this end they must be prepared to use self-control against the aimless straying of their passions, and patience and tenderness towards the realisation of the union when its time comes. Probably most youths and girls, at the age of romance, would easily appreciate this position; and it would bring to them a much more effective and natural idea of the sacredness of Marriage than they ever get from the artificial thunder of the Church and the State on the subject.

No doubt the suggestion of the mere possibility of any added freedom of choice and experience in the relations of the sexes will be very alarming to some people—but it is so, I think, not because they are at all ignorant that men already take to themselves considerable latitude, and that a distinct part of the undoubted evils that accompany that latitude springs from the fact that it is not recognised; not because they are ignorant that a vast number of respectable women and girls suffer frightful calamities and anguish by reason of the utter *inexperience* of sex in which they are brought up and have to live; but because such good people assume that any the least loosening of the formal barriers between the sexes must mean (and must be meant to mean) an utter dissolution of all ties, and the reign of mere licentiousness. They are convinced that nothing but the most unyielding and indeed exasperating straight-jacket can save society from madness and ruin.

To those, however, who can look facts in the face, and who see that as a matter of fact the *reality* of Marriage is coming more and more to be considered in the public mind in comparison with its *formalities*, the first thought will probably be one of congratulation that after such ages of treatment as a mere formality there should be any sense of the reality of the tie left; and the second will be the question how to give this reality its natural form and expression. Having satisfied ourselves that the formation of a more or less permanent double unit is—for our race and time—on the whole the natural and ascendant law of sex-union, slowly and with whatever exceptions establishing and enforcing itself independently of any artificial enactments that exist, then we shall not feel called upon to tear our hair or rend our garments at the prospect of added freedom for the operation of this force, but shall rather be anxious to consider how it may best *be* freed and given room for its reasonable development and growth.

I shall therefore devote the rest of the chapter to this question. And it will probably seem (looking back to what has already been said) that the points which most need consideration, as means to this end, are (1) the furtherance of the freedom and self-dependence of women; (2) the provision of some rational teaching, of heart and of head, for both sexes during the period of youth; (3) the recognition in marriage itself of a freer, more companionable, and less pettily exclusive relationship; and (4) the abrogation or modification of the present odious law which binds people together for *life*, without scruple, and in the most artificial and ill-assorted unions.

It must be admitted that the first point (1)

is of basic importance. As true Freedom cannot be without Love so true Love cannot be without Freedom. You cannot truly give yourself to another, unless you are master or mistress of yourself to begin with. Not only has the general *custom* of the self-dependence and self-ownership of women, in moral, social, and economic respects, to be gradually introduced, but the Law has to be altered in a variety of cases where it lags behind the public conscience in these matters—as in actual marriage, where it still leaves woman uncertain as to her rights over her own body, or in politics, where it still denies to her a voice in the framing of the statutes which are to bind her.

With regard to (2) hardly any one at this time of day would seriously doubt the desirability of giving adequate teaching to boys and girls. That is a point on which we have sufficiently touched, and which need not be further discussed here. But beyond this it is important, and especially perhaps, as things stand now, for girls—that each youth or girl should personally see enough of the other sex at an early period to be able to form some kind of judgment of his or her relation to that sex and to sex-matters generally. It is monstrous that the first case of sex-glamor—the true nature of which would be exposed by a little experience—should, perhaps for two people, decide the destinies of a life-time. Yet the more the sexes are kept apart, the more overwhelming does this glamor become, and the more ignorance is there, on either side, as to its nature. No doubt it is one of the great advantages of co-education of the sexes, that it tends to diminish these evils. Co-education, games and sports to some extent in common, and the doing away with the absurd superstition that because Corydon and Phyllis happen to kiss each other sitting on a gate, therefore they must live together all their lives, would soon mend matters considerably. Nor would a reasonable familiarity of this kind between the sexes in youth necessarily mean an increase of casual or clandestine sex-relations. But even if casualties did occur they would not be the fatal and unpardonable sins that they now—at least for girls—are considered to be. Though the recognition of anything like common pre-matrimonial sex-intercourse would probably be foreign to the temper of a northern nation; yet it is open to question whether Society here, in its mortal and fetichistic dread of the thing, has not, by keeping the young of both sexes in ignorance and darkness and seclusion from each other, created worse ills and suffering than it has prevented, and whether, by giving sexual acts so feverish an importance, it has not intensified the particular evil that it dreaded, rather than abated it.

In the next place (3) we come to the establishment in marriage itself of a freer and broader and more healthy relationship than generally exists at the present time. Attractive in some ways as the ideal of the exclusive attachment is, it runs the fatal risk, as we have already pointed out, of lapsing into a mere stagnant double selfishness. But, after all, Love is fed not by what it takes, but by what it gives; and the love of man and wife too must be fed by the love they give to others. If they cannot come out of their secluded haven to reach a hand to others, or even to give some boon of affection to those who need it more than themselves, or if they mistrust each other in doing so, then assuredly they are not very well fitted to live together.

A marriage, so free, so spontaneous, that it would allow of wide excursions of the pair from each other, in common or even in separate objects of work and interest, and yet would hold them all the time in the bond of absolute sympathy, would by its very freedom be all the more poignantly attractive, and by its very scope and breadth all the richer and more vital—would be in a sense indestructible; like the relation of two suns which, revolving in fluent and rebounding curves, only recede from each other in order to return again with renewed swiftness into close proximity—and which together blend their rays into the glory of one double star.

It has been the inability to see or understand this very simple truth that has largely contributed to the failure of the Monogamic union. The narrow physical passion of jealousy, the petty sense of private property in another person, social opinion, and legal enactments, have all converged to choke and suffocate wedded love in egoism, lust, and meanness. But surely it is not very difficult (for those who believe in the real thing) to imagine so sincere and natural a trust between man and wife that neither would be greatly alarmed at the other's friendship with a third person, nor conclude at once that it meant mere infidelity—or difficult even to imagine that such a friendship might be hailed as a gain by both parties. And if it is quite impossible (to some people) to see in such intimacies anything but a confusion of all sex-relations and a chaos of mere animal desire, we can only reply that this view exposes with fatal precision the kind of thoughts which our present marriage-system engenders. In order to suppose a rational marriage at all one must credit the parties concerned with *some* modicum of real affection, candor, common sense and self-control.

Withal seeing the remarkable and immense *variety* of love in human nature, when the feeling is really touched—how the love-offering of one person's soul and body is entirely different from that of another person's, so much so as almost to require another name—how one passion is predominantly physical, and another predominantly emotional, and another contemplative, or spiritual, or practical, or sentimental; how in one case it is jealous and exclusive, and in another hospitable and free, and so forth—it seems rash to lay down any very hard and fast general laws for the marriage-relation, or to insist that a real and honorable affection can only exist under this or that special form. It is probably through this fact of the variety of love that it does remain possible, in some cases, for married people to have intimacies with outsiders, and yet to continue perfectly true to each other; and in rare instances, for triune and other such relations to be permanently maintained.

We now come to the last consideration, namely (4) the modification of the present law of marriage. It is pretty clear that people will not much longer consent to pledge themselves irrevocably for life as at present. And indeed there are already plentiful indications of a growing change of practice. The more people come to recognise the sacredness and naturalness of the real union, the less will they be willing to bar themselves from this by a life-long and artificial contract made in their salad days. Hitherto the great bulwark of the existing institution has been the dependence of Women, which has given each woman a direct and most material interest in keeping up the supposed sanctity of the bond—and which has prevented a man of any generosity from proposing an alteration which would have the appearance of freeing himself at the cost of the woman; but as this fact of the dependence of women gradually dissolves out, and as the great fact of the spiritual nature of the true Marriage crystalises into more clearness—so will the formal bonds which bar the formation of the latter gradually break away and become of small import.

Love when felt at all deeply has an element of transcendentalism in it, which makes it the most natural thing in the world for the two lovers—even though drawn together by a passing sex-attraction—to swear eternal troth to each other; but there is something quite diabolic and mephistophelean in the practice of the Law, which creeping up behind, as it were, at this critical moment, and overhearing the two thus pledging themselves, claps its book together with a triumphant bang, and exclaims: "There now you are married and done for, for the rest of your natural lives."

What actual changes in Law and Custom the collective sense of society will bring about is a matter which in its detail we cannot of course foresee or determine. But that the drift will be, and must be, towards greater freedom, is pretty clear. Ideally speaking, it is plain that anything like a perfect union must have perfect freedom for its condition; and while it is quite supposable that a lover might out of the fulness of his heart *make* promises and give pledges, it is really almost inconceivable that anyone having that delicate and proud sense which marks deep feeling, could possibly *demand* a promise from his loved one. As there is undoubtedly a certain natural reticence in sex, so perhaps the most decent thing in true Marriage would be to say nothing, make no promises—either for a year or a lifetime. Promises are bad at any time, and when the heart is full silence befits it best. Practically, however, since a love of this kind is slow to be realised, since social custom is slow to change, and since the partial dependence and slavery of Woman must yet for a while continue, it is likely for such period that formal contracts of some kind will still be made; only these (it may be hoped) will lose their irrevocable and rigid character, and become in some degree adapted to the needs of the contracting parties.

Such contracts might of course, if adopted, be very various in respect to conjugal rights, conditions of termination, division of property, responsibility for and rights over children, etc. In some cases* possibly they might be looked upon as preliminary to a later and more permanent alliance; in others they would provide, for disastrous marriages, a remedy free from the inordinate scandals of the present Divorce Courts. It may, however, be said that rather than adopt any new system of contracts, public opinion in this country (Britain) would tend to a simple facilitation of Divorce, and that if the latter were made (with due provision for the children) to depend on mutual consent, it would become little more than an affair of registration, and the scandals of the proceeding would be avoided. In any case we think that marriage-contracts, if existing at all, must tend more and more to become matters of private arrangement as far as the relations of husband and wife are concerned, and that this is likely to happen in proportion as woman becomes more free, and

* *See* "Appendix."

therefore, more competent to act in her own right. It would be felt intolerable, in any decently constituted society, that the old blunderbuss of the Law should interfere in the delicate relations of wedded life. As it is to-day the situation is most absurd. On the one hand, having been constituted from times back in favor of the male, the Law still gives to the husband barbarous rights over the person of his spouse; on the other hand, to compensate for this, it rushes in with the farcicalities of Breach of Promise; and in any case, having once pronounced its benediction over a pair—however hateful the alliance may turn out to be to both parties, and however obvious its failure to the whole world—the stupid old thing blinks owlishly on at its own work, and professes itself totally unable to undo the knot which once it tied!

The only point where there is a permanent ground for State interference—and where indeed there is no doubt that the public authority should in some way make itself felt—is in the matter of the children resulting from any alliance. Here the relation of the pair ceases to be private and becomes social; and the interests of the child itself, and of the nation whose future citizen the child is, have to be safe-guarded. Any contracts, or any proposals of divorce, before they could be sanctioned by the public authority, would have to contain satisfactory provisions for the care and maintenance of the children in such casualties as might ensue; nor ought there to be maintained any legal distinction between "natural" and "legitimate" children, since it is clear that whatever individuals or society at large may, in the former case, think of the conduct of the parents, no disability should on that account accrue to the child, nor should the parents (if identifiable) be able to escape their full responsibility for bringing it into the world. If those good people who make such a terrific outcry against folk entering into married life without going through all the abracadabra of the Law, *on account of the children,* would try and get the law altered so as to give illegitimate children the same *status* and claim on their parents as legitimate children, it would show more genuinely for their anxiety about the children, and would really be doing something in the interests of positive morality.

If it be objected that private contracts, or such facilitations of Divorce as here spoken of, would simply lead to frivolous experimental relationships entered into and broken-off *ad infinitum,* it must be remembered that the responsibility for due rearing and maintenance of children must give serious pause to such a career; and that to suppose that any great mass of people would find their good in a kind of matrimonial game of General Post is to suppose that the mass of the people have really never acquired or been taught the rudiments of common sense in such matters—is to suppose a case for which there would hardly be a parallel in the customs of any nation or tribe that we know of.

In conclusion, it is evident that no very great change for the better in marriage relations can take place except as the accompaniment of deep-lying changes in Society at large; and that alterations in the Law alone will effect but a limited improvement. Indeed it is not very likely, as long as the present commercial order of society lasts, that the existing Marriage-laws—founded as they are on the idea of property—*will* be very radically altered, though they may be to some extent. More likely is it that, underneath the law, the common practice will slide forward into newer customs. With the rise of the new society which is already outlining itself within the structure of the old, many of the difficulties and bugbears, that at present seem to stand in the way of a more healthy relation between the sexes, will of themselves disappear.

It must be acknowledged, however, that though a gradual broadening out and humanising of Law and Custom are quite necessary, it cannot fairly be charged against these ancient tyrants that they are responsible for *all* the troubles connected with sex. There are millions of people to-day who never could marry happily—however favorable the conditions might be—simply because their natures do not contain in sufficient strength the elements of loving surrender to another; and, as long as the human heart is what it is, there will be natural tragedies arising from the willingness or unwillingness of one person to release another when the former finds that his or her love is not returned.* While it is quite necessary that these natural tragedies should not be complicated and multiplied by needless legal interference—complicated into the numberless artificial tragedies which are so exasperating when represented on the stage or in romance, and so saddening when witnessed in real life—still we may acknowledge that, short of the millennium, they will always be with us,

* Perhaps one of the most sombre and inscrutable of these natural tragedies lies, for Woman, in the fact that the man to whom she first surrenders her body often acquires for her (whatever his character may be) so profound and inalienable a claim upon her heart. While, either for man or woman, it is almost impossible to thoroughly understand their own nature, or that of others, till they have had sex-experience, it happens so that in the case of woman the experience which should thus give the power of choice is frequently the very one which seals her destiny. It reveals to her, as at a glance, the tragedy of a life-time which lies before her, and yet which she cannot do other than accept.

and that no institution of marriage, or absence of institution, will rid us of them. That entire and unswerving refusal to "cage" another person, or to accept an affection not perfectly free and spontaneous, which will, we are fain to think, be always more and more the mark of human love, must inevitably bring its own price of mortal suffering with it; yet the Love so gained, whether in the individual or in society, will be found in the end to be worth the pang—and as far beyond the other love, as is the wild bird of Paradise that comes to feed out of our hands unbidden more lovely than the prisoner we shut with draggled wings behind the bars. Love is doubtless the last and most difficult lesson that humanity has to learn; in a sense it underlies all the others. Perhaps the time has come for the modern nations when, ceasing to be children, they may even try to learn it.

THE INTERMEDIATE SEX

IN late years (and since the arrival of the New Woman amongst us) many things in the relation of men and women to each other have altered, or at any rate become clearer. The growing sense of equality in habits and customs—university studies, art, music, politics, the bicycle, etc.—all these things have brought about a rapprochement between the sexes. If the modern woman is a little more masculine in some ways than her predecessor, the modern man (it is to be hoped), while by no means effeminate, is a little more sensitive in temperament and artistic in feeling than the original John Bull. It is beginning to be recognised that the sexes do not or should not normally form two groups hopelessly isolated in habit and feeling from each other, but that they rather represent the two poles of *one* group—which is the human race; so that while certainly the extreme specimens at either pole are vastly divergent, there are great numbers in the middle region who (though differing corporeally as men and women), are by emotion and temperament very near to each other. We all know women with a strong dash of the masculine temperament, and we all know men whose almost feminine sensibility and intuition seem to belie their bodily form. Nature, it might appear, in mixing the elements which go to compose each individual, does not always keep her two groups of ingredients—which represent the two sexes—properly apart, but often throws them crosswise in a somewhat baffling manner, now this way and now that; yet wisely, we must think—for if a severe distinction of elements were always maintained, the two sexes would soon drift into far latitudes and absolutely cease to understand each other. As it is, there are some remarkable and (we think) indispensable types of character, in whom there is such a union or balance of the feminine and masculine qualities that these people become to a great extent the interpreters of men and women to each other.

There is another point which has become clearer of late. For as people are beginning to see that the sexes form in a certain sense a continuous group, so they are beginning to see that Love and Friendship—which have been so often set apart from each other as things distinct—are in reality closely related and shade imperceptibly into each other. Women are beginning to demand that Marriage shall mean Friendship as well as Passion; that a comrade-like Equality shall be included in the word Love; and it is recognised that from the one extreme of a "Platonic" friendship (generally between persons of the same sex) up to the other extreme of passionate love (generally between persons of opposite sex) no hard and fast line can at any point be drawn effectively separating the different kinds of attachment. We know, in fact, of Friendships so romantic in sentiment that they verge into love; we know of Loves so intellectual and spiritual that they hardly dwell in the sphere of Passion.

A moment's thought will show that the general conceptions indicated above—if anywhere near the truth—point to an immense diversity of human temperament and character in matters relating to sex and love; but though such diversity has probably always existed, it has only in comparatively recent times become a subject of study.

More than thirty years ago, however, an Austrian writer, K. H. Ulrichs, drew attention in a series of pamphlets (*Memnon, Ara Spei, Inclusa,* etc.) to the existence of a class of people who strongly illustrate the above remarks, and with whom specially this paper is concerned. He pointed out that there were people born in such a position—as it were on the dividing line between the sexes—that while belonging distinctly to one sex as far as their bodies are concerned they may be said to belong *mentally* and *emotionally* to the other; that there were men, for instance, who might be described as of feminine soul enclosed in a male body (*anima muliebris in corpore virili inclusa*), or in other cases, women whose definition would be just the reverse. And he maintained that this doubleness of nature was to a great extent proved by the special direction of their love-sentiment. For in such cases, as indeed might be expected, the (apparently) masculine person instead of forming a love-union with a female tended to contract romantic friendships with one of his own sex; while the apparently feminine would, instead of marrying in the usual way, devote herself to the love of another feminine.

People of this kind (*i. e.*, having this special variation of the love-sentiment) he called Urnings;* and though we are not obliged to accept his theory about the crosswise connexion between "soul" and "body," since at best these words are somewhat vague and indefinite; yet his work was important because it was one of the first attempts, in modern times, to recognise the existence of

* From *Uranos*, heaven; his idea being that the Urning-love was of a higher order than the ordinary attachment.

what might be called an Intermediate sex, and to give at any rate *some* explanation of it.*

Since that time the subject has been widely studied and written about by scientific men and others, especially on the Continent (though in England and the United States, it is still comparatively unknown), and by means of an extended observation of present-day cases, as well as the indirect testimony of the history and literature of past times, quite a body of general conclusions has been arrived at—of which I propose in the following pages to give some slight account.

Contrary to the general impression, one of the first points that emerges from this study is that "Urnings," or Uranians, are by no means so very rare; but that they form, beneath the surface of society, a large class. It remains difficult, however, to get an exact statement of their numbers; and this for more than one reason—partly because, owing to the want of any general understanding of their case, these folk tend to conceal their true feelings from all but their own kind, and indeed often deliberately act in such a manner as to lead the world astray—(whence it arises

* Charles G. Leland ("Hans Breitmann") in his book *The Alternate Sex* (1904), insists much on the frequent combination of the characteristics of both sexes in remarkable men and women, and has a chapter on "The Female Mind in Man," and another on "The Male Intellect in Woman."

that a normal man living in a certain society will often refuse to believe that there is a single Urning in the circle of his acquaintance, while one of the latter, or one that understands the nature, living in the same society, can count perhaps a score or more)—and partly because it is indubitable that the numbers do vary very greatly, not only in different countries, but even in different classes in the same country; the consequence of all this being that we have estimates differing very widely from each other. Dr. Grabowsky, a well-known writer in Germany, quotes figures (which we think must be exaggerated) as high as 1 man in every 22, while Dr. Albert Moll (*Die Conträre Sexual-empfindung,* chap. 3), gives estimates varying from 1 in every 50 to as low as 1 in every 500.* These figures apply to such as are exclusively of the said nature, *i. e.*, to those whose deepest feelings of love and friendship go out only to persons of their own sex. Of course, if in addition are included those double-natured people (of whom there is a great number) who experience the normal attachment, with the homogenic tendency in less or greater degree superadded, the estimates must be greatly higher.

---

* Some late statistical inquiries (see *Statistische Untersuchungen,* Dr. M. Hirschfeld, Leipzig, 1904) yield 1.5 to 2.0 per cent. as a probable ratio.

In the second place it emerges (also contrary to the general impression) that men and women of the exclusive Uranian type are by no means necessarily morbid in any way—unless, indeed, their peculiar temperament be pronounced in itself morbid. Formerly it was assumed, as a matter of course, that the type was merely a result of disease and degeneration; but now with the examination of the actual facts it appears that, on the contrary, many are fine, healthy specimens of their sex, muscular and well-developed in body, of powerful brain, high standard of conduct, and with nothing abnormal or morbid of any kind observable in their physical structure or constitution. This is, of course, not true of all, and there still remain a certain number of cases of weakly type to support the neuropathic view. Yet it is very noticeable that this view is much less insisted on by the later writers than by the earlier. It is also worth noticing that it is now acknowledged that even in the most healthy cases the special affectional temperament of the "Intermediate" is, as a rule, ineradicable; so much so that when (as in not a few instances) such men and women, from social or other considerations, have forced themselves to marry, and even have children, they have still not been able to overcome their own bias, or the leaning after all of their life-attachment to some friend of their own sex.

This subject, though obviously one of considerable interest and importance, has been hitherto, as I have pointed out, but little discussed in this country, partly owing to a certain amount of doubt and distrust which has, not unnaturally perhaps, surrounded it. And certainly if the men and women born with the tendency in question were only exceedingly rare, though it would not be fair on that account to ignore them, yet it would hardly be necessary to dwell at great length on their case. But as the class is really, on any computation, numerous, it becomes a duty for society not only to understand them but to help them to understand themselves.

For there is no doubt that in many cases people of this kind suffer a good deal from their own temperament—and yet after all it is possible that they may have an important part to play in the evolution of the race. Anyone who realises what Love is, the dedication of the heart, so profound, so absorbing, so mysterious, so imperative, and always just in the noblest natures so strong, cannot fail to see how difficult, how tragic even, must often be the fate of those whose deepest feelings are destined from the earliest days to be a riddle and a stumbling-block, unexplained to themselves, passed over in silence by others. To call people of such temperament "morbid," and so forth, is of no use. Such a term is, in fact, absurdly inapplicable to many, who are amongst the most active, the most amiable and accepted members of society; besides, it forms no solution of the problem in question, and only amounts to marking down for disparagement a fellow-creature who has already considerable difficulties to contend with. Says Dr. Moll, "Anyone who has seen many Urnings will probably admit that they form a by no means enervated human group; on the contrary, one finds powerful, healthy-looking folk among them"; but in the very next sentence he says that they "suffer severely" from the way they are regarded; and in the manifesto of a considerable community of such people in Germany occur these words, "The rays of sunshine in the night of our existence are so rare, that we are responsive and deeply grateful for the least movement, for every single voice that speaks in our favor in the forum of mankind."*

In dealing with this class of folk, then, while I do not deny that they present a difficult problem, I think that just for that very reason their case needs discussion. It would be a great mis-

* See De Joux, *Die Enterbten des Liebes-glückes* (Leipzig, 1893), p. 21.

take to suppose that their attachments are necessarily sexual, or connected with sexual acts. On the contrary (as abundant evidence shows), they are often purely emotional in their character; and to confuse Uranians (as is so often done) with libertines having no law but curiosity in self-indulgence is to do them a great wrong. At the same time, it is evident that their special temperament may sometimes cause them difficulty in regard to their sexual relations. Into this subject we need not now enter. But we may point out how hard it is, especially for the young among them, that a veil of complete silence should be drawn over the subject, leading to the most painful misunderstandings, and perversions and confusions of mind; and that there should be no hint of guidance; nor any recognition of the solitary and really serious inner struggles they may have to face! If the problem is a difficult one—as it undoubtedly is—the fate of those people is already hard who have to meet it in their own persons, without their suffering in addition from the refusal of society to give them any help. It is partly for these reasons, and to throw a little light where it may be needed, that I have thought it might be advisable in this paper simply to give a few general characteristics of the Intermediate types.

As indicated then already, in bodily structure there is, as a rule, nothing to distinguish the subjects of our discussion from ordinary men and women; but if we take the general mental characteristics it appears from almost universal testimony that the male tends to be of a rather gentle, emotional disposition—with defects, if such exist, in the direction of subtlety, evasiveness, timidity, vanity, etc.; while the female is just the opposite—fiery, active, bold and truthful, with defects running to brusqueness and coarseness. Moreover, the mind of the former is generally intuitive and instinctive in its perceptions, with more or less of artistic feeling; while the mind of the latter is more logical, scientific, and precise than usual with the normal woman. So marked indeed are these general characteristics that sometimes by means of them (though not an infallible guide) the nature of the boy or girl can be detected in childhood, before full development has taken place; and needless to say, it may often be very important to be able to do this.

It was no doubt in consequence of the observation of these signs that K. H. Ulrichs proposed his theory; and though the theory, as we have said, does not by any means meet *all* the facts, still it is perhaps not without merit, and may be worth bearing in mind.

In the case, for instance, of a woman of this temperament (defined we suppose as "a male soul in a female body") the theory helps us to understand how it might be possible for her to fall *bona fide* in love with another woman. Krafft-Ebing, of Vienna, gives* the case of a lady (A.), 28 years of age, who fell deeply in love with a younger one (B.). "I loved her divinely," she said. They lived together, and the union lasted four years, but was then broken by the marriage of B. A. suffered in consequence from frightful depression; but in the end—though without real love—got married herself. Her depression, however, only increased, and deepened into illness. The doctors, when consulted, said that all would be well if she could only have a child. The husband, who loved his wife sincerely, could not understand her enigmatic behavior. She was friendly to him, suffered his caresses, but for days afterwards remained "dull, exhausted, plagued with irritation of the spine, and nervous." Presently a journey of the married pair led to another meeting with the female friend—who had now been wedded (but also unhappily) for three years. "Both ladies trembled with joy and excitement as they fell into each other's arms, and were thenceforth inseparable. The man found that

* *Psychopathia Sexualis,* 7th ed., p. 276.

this friendship relation was a singular one, and hastened the departure. When the opportunity occurred, he convinced himself from the correspondence between his wife and her 'friend' that their letters were exactly like those of two lovers."

It appears that the loves of such women are often very intense, and (as also in the case of male Urnings) life-long. Both classes feel themselves blessed when they love happily. Nevertheless, to many of them it is a painful fact that—in consequence of their peculiar temperament—they are, though fond of children, not in the position to found a family.

We have so far limited ourselves to some very general characteristics of the Intermediate race. It may help to clear and fix our ideas if we now describe more in detail, first, what may be called the extreme and exaggerated types of the race, and then the more normal and perfect types. By doing so we shall get a more definite and concrete view of our subject.

In the first place, then, the extreme specimens—as in most cases of extremes—are not particularly attractive, sometimes quite the reverse. In the male of this kind we have a distinctly effeminate type, sentimental, lackadaisical, mincing in gait and manners, something of a chatterbox, skilful at the needle and in woman's work, sometimes taking pleasure in dressing in woman's clothes; his figure not unfrequently betraying a tendency towards the feminine, large at the hips, supple, not muscular, the face wanting in hair, the voice inclined to be high-pitched, etc.; while his dwelling-room is orderly in the extreme, even natty, and choice of decoration and perfume. His affection too is often feminine in character, clinging, dependent and jealous, as of one desiring to be loved almost more than to love.*

On the other hand, as the extreme type of the homogenic female, we have a rather markedly aggressive person, of strong passions, masculine manners and movements, practical in the conduct of life, sensuous rather than sentimental in love, often untidy, and *outré* in attire;† her figure muscular, her voice rather low in pitch; her dwelling-room decorated with sporting-scenes, pistols, etc., and not without a suspicion of the fragrant weed in the atmosphere; while her love (generally to rather soft and feminine specimens of her own sex) is often a sort of furor, similar to the ordinary masculine love, and at times almost uncontrollable.

* A good deal in this description may remind readers of history of the habits and character of Henry III. of France.

† Perhaps like Queen Christine of Sweden, who rode across Europe, on her visit to Italy, in jack-boots and sitting astride of her horse. It is said that she shook the Pope's hand, on seeing him, so heartily that the doctor had to attend to it afterwards!

These are types which, on account of their salience, everyone will recognise more or less. Naturally, when they occur, they excite a good deal of attention, and it is not an uncommon impression that most persons of the homogenic nature belong to either one or other of these classes. But in reality, of course, these extreme developments are rare, and for the most part the temperament in question is embodied in men and women of quite normal and unsensational exterior.

Speaking of the subject, and the connection between effeminateness and the homogenic nature in men, Dr. Moll says: "It is, however, as well to point out at the outset that effeminacy does not by any means show itself in all Urnings. Though one may find this or that indication in a great number of cases, yet it cannot be denied that a very large percentage, perhaps by far the majority of them, do *not* exhibit pronounced effeminacy." And it may be supposed that we may draw the same conclusion with regard to women of this class—namely, that the majority of them do not exhibit pronounced masculine habits. In fact, while these extreme cases are of the greatest value from a scientific point of view as marking tendencies and limits of development in certain directions, it would be a serious mistake to look upon them as representative cases of the whole phases of human evolution concerned.

If now we come to what may be called the more normal type of the Uranian man, we find a man who, while possessing thoroughly masculine powers of mind and body, combines with them the tenderer and more emotional soul-nature of the woman—and sometimes to a remarkable degree. Such men, as said, are often muscular and well-built, and not distinguishable in exterior structure and the carriage of body from others of their own sex; but emotionally they are extremely complex, tender, sensitive, pitiful and loving, "full of storm and stress, of ferment and fluctuation" of the heart; the logical faculty may or may not, in their case, be well-developed, but intuition is always strong; like women they read characters at a glance, and know, without knowing how, what is passing in the minds of others; for nursing and waiting on the needs of others they have often a peculiar gift; at the bottom lies the artist-nature, with the artist's sensibility and perception. Such an one is often a dreamer, of brooding reserved habits, often a musician, or a man of culture, courted in society, which nevertheless does not understand him—though sometimes a child of the people, without any culture, but almost always with a peculiar inborn refinement. De Joux, who speaks on the whole favorably of Uranian men and women, says of the former: "They are enthusiastic for poetry and music, are often eminently skilful in the fine arts, and are overcome with emotion and sympathy at the least sad occurrence. Their sensitiveness, their endless tenderness for children, their love of flowers, their great pity for beggars and crippled folk are truly womanly." And in another passage he indicates the artist-nature, when he says: "The nerve-system of many an Urning is the finest and the most complicated musical instrument in the service of the interior personality that can be imagined."

It would seem probable that the attachment of such an one is of a very tender and profound character; indeed, it is possible that in this class of men we have the love sentiment in one of its most perfect forms—a form in which from the necessities of the situation the sensuous element, though present, is exquisitely subordinated to the spiritual. Says one writer on this subject, a Swiss, "Happy indeed is that man who has won a real Urning for his friend—he walks on roses, without ever having to fear the thorns"; and he adds, "Can there ever be a more perfect sick-nurse than an Urning?" And though these are *ex parte* utterances, we may believe that there is an appreciable grain of truth in them. Another writer, quoted by De Joux, speaks to somewhat the same effect, and may perhaps be received in a similar spirit. "We form," he says, "a peculiar aristocracy of modest spirits, of good and refined habit, and in many masculine circles are the representatives of the higher mental and artistic element. In us dreamers and enthusiasts lies the continual counterpoise to the sheer masculine portion of society—inclining, as it always does, to mere restless greed of gain and material sensual pleasures."

That men of this kind despise women, though a not uncommon belief, is one which hardly appears to be justified. Indeed, though naturally not inclined to "fall in love" in this direction, such men are by their nature drawn rather near to women, and it would seem that they often feel a singular appreciation and understanding of the emotional needs and destinies of the other sex, leading in many cases to a genuine though what is called a "Platonic" friendship. There is little doubt that they are often instinctively sought after by women, who, without suspecting the real cause, are conscious of a sympathetic chord in the homogenic which they miss in the normal man. To quote De Joux once more: "It would be a mistake to suppose that all

Urnings must be women-haters. Quite the contrary. They are not seldom the faithfulest friends, the truest allies, and most convinced defenders of women."

To come now to the more normal and perfect specimens of the homogenic *woman,* we find a type in which the body is thoroughly feminine and gracious, with the rondure and fulness of the female form, and the continence and aptness of its movements, but in which the inner nature is to a great extent masculine; a temperament active, brave, originative, somewhat decisive, not too emotional; fond of outdoor life, of games and sports, of science, politics, or even business; good at organisation, and well-pleased with positions of responsibility, sometimes indeed making an excellent and generous leader. Such a woman, it is easily seen, from her special combination of qualities, is often fitted for remarkable work, in professional life, or as manageress of institutions, or even as ruler of a country. Her love goes out to younger and more feminine natures than her own; it is a powerful passion, almost of heroic type, and capable of inspiring to great deeds; and when held duly in leash may sometimes become an invaluable force in the teaching and training of girlhood, or in the creation of a school of thought or action among women. Many a Santa Clara, or abbess-founder of religious houses, has probably been a woman of this type; and in all times such women—not being bound to men by the ordinary ties—have been able to work the more freely for the interests of their sex, a cause to which their own temperament impels them to devote themselves *con amore*.

I have now sketched—very briefly and inadequately it is true—both the extreme types and the more healthy types of the "Intermediate" man and woman: types which can be verified from history and literature, though more certainly and satisfactorily perhaps from actual life around us. And unfamiliar though the subject is, it begins to appear that it is one which modern thought and science will have to face. Of the latter and more normal types it may be said that they exist, and have always existed, in considerable abundance, and from that circumstance alone there is a strong probability that they have their place and purpose. As pointed out there is no particular indication of morbidity about them, unless the special nature of their love-sentiment be itself accounted morbid; and in the alienation of the sexes from each other, of which complaint is so often made to-day, it must be admitted that they do much to fill the gap.

The instinctive artistic nature of the male of

this class, his sensitive spirit, his wavelike emotional temperament, combined with hardihood of intellect and body; and the frank, free nature of the female, her masculine independence and strength wedded to thoroughly feminine grace of form and manner; may be said to give them both, through their double nature, command of life in all its phases, and a certain freemasonry of the secrets of the two sexes which may well favor their function as reconcilers and interpreters. Certainly it is remarkable that some of the world's greatest leaders and artists have been dowered either wholly or in part with the Uranian temperament—as in the cases of Michael Angelo, Shakespeare, Marlowe, Alexander the Great, Julius Caesar, or, among women, Christine of Sweden, Sappho the poetess, and others.

THE FREE SOCIETY

TAKING, finally, a somewhat wider outlook over the whole subject of the most intimate human relations than was feasible in the foregoing chapters, we may make a few general remarks.

One of the great difficulties in the way of arriving at any general understanding on questions of sex—and one which we have already had occasion to note—is the extraordinary diversity of feeling and temperament which exists in these matters. Needless to say, this is increased by the reserve, natural or artificial, which so seldom allows people to express their sentiments quite freely. In the great ocean there are so many currents, cold and warm, fresh, and salt, and brackish; and each one thinks that the current in which he lives is the whole ocean. The man of the world hardly understands, certainly does not sympathise with, the recluse or ascetic—and the want of appreciation is generally returned; the maternal, the sexual, and the philanthropic woman, are all somewhat unintelligible to each other; the average male and the average female approach the great passion from totally different sides, and are continually at odds over it; and again both of these great sections of humanity fail entirely to understand that other and well-marked class of persons whose love-attraction is (inborn) towards their own sex, and indeed hardly recognise the existence of such a class, although as a matter of fact it is a large and important one in every community. In fact, all these differences have hitherto been so little the subject of impartial study that we are still amazingly in the dark about them.

When we look back to History, and the various customs of the world in different races and tribes and at different periods of time, we seem to see these natural divergencies of human temperament reflected in the extraordinary diversity of practices that have obtained and been recognised. We see that, in some cases, the worship of sex took its place beside the worship of the gods; and—what appears equally strange—that the orgiastic rites and saturnalia of the early world were intimately connected with religious feeling; we find that, in other cases, asceticism and chastity and every denial of the flesh were glorified and looked upon as providing the only way to the heavenly kingdom; we discover that marriage has been instituted and defined and sanctioned in endless forms, each looked upon as the only moral and possible form in its own time and country; and that the position of women under these different conditions has varied in the most remarkable way—that in some of the primitive societies where group-marriages* of one kind or another prevailed their dignity and influence were of the highest, that under some forms of Monogamy, as among the Nagas of Bengal,† women have been abjectly degraded, while under other forms, as in Ancient Egypt and the later Roman Empire, they have been treated with respect; and so forth. We cannot fail, I say, to recognise the enormous diversity of practice which has existed over the world in this matter of the relations of the sexes; nor, I may add, can we venture—if we possess any sense of humanity—to put our finger down finally on any one custom or institution, and say, Here alone is the right way.

On the contrary, it seems to me probable that, broadly speaking, a really free Society will accept and make use of all that has gone before. If, as we have suggested, historical forms and cus-

* See Note on the Primitive Group-marriage, *infra*.

† Letourneau ("Evolution of Marriage," p. 173) mentions also among the inferior races who have adopted Monogamy the Veddahs of Ceylon, the Bochimans of S. Africa, and the Kurnais of Australia.

toms are the indication of tendencies and instincts which still exist among us, then the question is, not the extinction of these tendencies, but the finding of the right place and really rational expression for them. That the various customs of past social life do subsist on beneath the surface of modern society, we know well enough; and it seems likely that society in the future will have to recognise and to a certain extent transform these.

In fact, in recognising it will inevitably transform, for it will bring them out from darkness into light, and from the old conditions and surroundings of the past societies into the new conditions of the modern. Polygamy, for instance, or some related form of union, supposing it really did spontaneously and naturally arise in a society which gave perfect freedom and independence to women in their relation to men, would be completely different in character from the old-world polygamy, and would cease to act as a degrading influence on women, since it would be the spontaneous expression of their attachment to each other and to a common husband; Monogamy, under similar circumstances, would lose its narrowness and stuffiness; and the life of the Hetaira, that is of the woman who choses to be the companion of more than one man, might not be without dignity, honor, and sincere attachment.

Again it is easy to see, if the sense of cleanness in sex ever does come in, if the physical body ever becomes clean (which it certainly is not now-a-days), clean and beautiful and accepted, within and without—and this, of course, it can only be through a totally changed method of life, through pure and clean food, nakedness to a large extent, and a kind of saturation with the free air and light of heaven; and if the mental and moral relation ever becomes clean, which can only be with the freedom of woman and the sincerity of man, and so forth; it is easy to see how entirely all this would alter our criticism of the various sex-relations, and our estimate of their place and fitness.

In the wild and even bacchanalian festivals of all the earlier nations, there was an element of Nature-sex-mysticism which has become lost in modern times, or quite unclean and depraved; yet we cannot but see that this element is a vital and deep-lying one in humanity, and in some form or other will probably reassert itself. On the other hand, in the Monkish and other ascetic movements of Christian or pre-Christian times, with their efforts towards a proud ascendancy over the body, there was (commonly sneered at though it may be in the modern West) an equally vital and important truth,* which will have to be rehabilitated. The practices of former races and times, however anomalous they may sometimes appear to us, were after all in the main the expression of needs and desires which *had* their place there, even though overlaid and suppressed beneath existing convention; and who knows, in all the stifled longings of thousands and thousands of hearts, how the great broad soul of Humanity—which reaches to and accepts all times and races—is still ever asserting herself and swelling against the petty bonds of this or that age? The nearer Society comes to its freedom and majority the more lovingly will it embrace this great soul within it, and recognising in all the customs of the past the partial efforts of that soul to its own fulfillment will refuse to deny them, but rather seek, by acceptance and reunion, to transform and illumine them all.

Possibly, to some, these remarks will only suggest a return to general confusion and promiscuity; and of course to such people they will seem inconsistent with what has been said before on the subject of the real Marriage and the tendency of human beings, as society evolves, to seek more and more sincerely a life-long union with

* See Remarks on the Early Star and Sex Worships, *infra.*

their chosen mate; but no one who thinks twice about the matter could well make this mistake. For the latter tendency, that namely "from confusion to distinction," is in reality the tendency of all evolution, and cannot be set aside. It is in the very nature of Love that as it realises its own aim it should rivet always more and more towards a durable and distinct relationship, nor rest till the permanent mate and equal is found. As human beings progress their relations to each other must become much *more* definite and distinct instead of less so—and there is no likelihood of society in its onward march lapsing backward, so to speak, to formlessness again.

But it is just the advantage of this onward movement towards definiteness that it allows—as in the evolution of all organic life—of more and more *differentiation* as the life rises higher in the scale of existence. If society should at any future time recognise—as we think likely it will do—the variety of needs of the human heart and of human beings, it will not therefore confuse them, but will see that these different needs indicate different functions, all of which may have their place and purpose. If it has the good sense to tolerate a Nature-festival now and then, and a certain amount of animalism let loose, it will not be so foolish as to be unable to distinguish this from the deep delight and happiness of a permanent spiritual mating; or if it recognises in some case, a woman's temporary alliance with a man for the sake of obtaining a much-needed child, it will not therefore be so silly as to mark her down for life as a common harlot. It will allow in fact that there *are* different forms and functions of the love-sentiment, and while really believing that a life-long comradeship (possibly with little of the sexual in it), is the most satisfying form, will see that a cast-iron Marriage-custom which, as to-day, expects two people either to live eternally in the same house and sit on opposite sides of the same table, or else to be strangers to each other—and which only recognises two sorts of intimacy, orthodox and criminal, wedded and adulterous—is itself the source of perpetual confusion and misapprehension.

No doubt the Freedom of Society in this sense, and the possibility of a human life which shall be the fluid and ever-responsive embodiment of true Love in all its variety of manifestation, goes with the Freedom of Society in the economic sense. When mankind has solved the industrial problem so far that the products of our huge mechanical forces have become a common heritage, and no man or woman is the property-slave of another, then some of the causes which compel prostitution, property-marriage, and other perversions of affection, will have disappeared; and in such economically free society human unions may at last take place according to their own inner and true laws.

Hitherto we have hardly thought whether there were any inner laws or not; our thoughts have been fixed on the outer; and the Science of Love, if it may so be called, has been strangely neglected. Yet if, putting aside for a moment all convention and custom, one will look quietly within himself, he will perceive that there are most distinct and inviolable inner forces, binding him by different ties to different people, and with different and inevitable results according to the quality and the nature of the affection bestowed—that there is in fact in that world of the heart a kind of cosmical harmony and variety, and an order almost astronomical.

This is noticeably true of what may be called the planetary law of distances in the relation of people to one another. For of some of the circle of one's acquaintance it may be said that one loves them cordially at a hundred miles' distance; of others that they are dear friends at a mile; while others again are indispensable far nearer than that. If by any chance the friend whose planetary distance is a mile is forced into closer quarters, the only result is a violent development of repulsion and centrifugal force, by which probably he is carried even beyond his normal distance, till such time as he settles down into his right place; while on the other hand if we are separated for a season from one who by right is very near and who we know belongs to us, we can bide our time, knowing that the forces of return will increase with the separation. How marked and definite these personal distances are may be gathered from considering how largely the art of life consists in finding and *keeping* them, and how much trouble arises from their confusion, and from the way in which we often only find them out after much blundering and suffering and mutual recrimination.

So marked indeed are these and other such laws that they sometimes suggest that there really is a cosmic world of souls, to which we all belong—a world of souls whose relations are eternal and clearly-defined; and that our terrestrial relations are merely the working-out and expression of far antecedent and unmodifiable facts—an idea which for many people is corroborated by the curious way in which, often at the very first sight, they become aware of their exact relation to a new-comer. In some cases this brings with it a strange sense of previous intimacy, hard to explain; and in other cases, not so intimate, it still will seem to fix almost instantaneously the exact propinquity of the relation—so that though in succeeding years, or even decades of years, the mutual acquaintanceship may work itself out with all sorts of interesting and even unexpected developments and episodes, yet this *mean distance* does not vary during the whole time, so to speak, by a single hair's breadth.

Is it possible, we may ask (in the light of such experiences), that there really *is* a Free Society in another and deeper sense than that hitherto suggested—a society to which we all in our inmost selves consciously or unconsciously belong—the Rose of souls that Dante beheld in Paradise, whose every petal is an individual, and an individual only through its union with all the rest—the early Church's dream, of an eternal Fellowship in heaven and on earth—the Prototype of all the brotherhoods and communities that exist on this or any planet; and that the innumerable selves of men, united in the one Self, members of it and of one another (like the members of the body) stand in eternal and glorious relationship bound indissolubly together? We know of course that the reality of things cannot be adequately expressed by such phrases as these, or by any phrases, yet possibly some such conception comes as near the truth as any *one* conception can; and, making use of it, we may think that our earthly relations are a continual attempt—through much blindness and ineffectualness and failure—to feel after and to find these true and permanent relations to others.

Surely in some subtle way if one person sincerely love another, heart and soul, that other becomes a part of the lover, indissolubly wrought into his being.* Mentally the two grow and become compact together. No thought that the lover thinks, no scene that he looks on, but the impress of his loved one in some way is on it—so that as long as he exists (here or anywhere) with his most intimate self that other is threaded and twined inseparably. So clinging is the relation. Perhaps in the outer world we do not always see such relations quite clear, and we think when death or other cause removes the visible form from us that the hour of parting has come. But in the inner world it is clear enough, and we divine that we and our mate are only two little petals that grow near each other on the great Flower of Eternity; and that it is because we are near each other in that unchanging world, that

* Perhaps this accounts for the feeling, which so many have experienced, that a great love, even though not apparently returned, *justifies itself*, and *has* its fruition in its own time and its own way.

in the world of change our mortal selves are drawn together, and will be drawn always, wherever and whenever they may meet.

But since the petals of the immortal Flower are by myriads and myriads, so have we endless lessons of soul-relationship to learn—some most intimate, others doubtless less so, but all fair and perfect—so soon as we have discovered *what* these relationships really are, and are in no confusion of mind about them. For even those that are most distant are desirable, and have the germ of love in them, so soon as they are touched by the spirit of Truth (which means the fearless statement of the life which is in us, in poise against the similar statement of life in others); since, indeed, the spirit of Truth *is* the life of the whole, and only the other side of that Love which binds the whole together.

Looking at things in this light it would seem to us that the ideal of terrestrial society for which we naturally strive is that which would embody best these enduring and deep-seated relations of human souls; and that every society, as far as it is human and capable of holding together, is in its degree a reflection of the celestial City. Never is the essential, real, Society quite embodied in any mundane Utopia, but ever through human history is it working unconsciously in the midst of mortal affairs and impelling towards an expression of itself.

At any rate, and however all this may be, the conclusion is that the *inner* laws in these matters—the inner laws of the sex-passion, of love, and of all human relationship—must gradually appear and take the lead, since they alone are the powers which can create and uphold a rational society; and that the outer laws—since they are dead and lifeless things—must inevitably disappear. Real love is only possible in the freedom of society; and freedom is only possible when love is a reality. The subjection of sex-relations to legal conventions is an intolerable bondage, but of course it is a bondage inescapable as long as people are slaves to a merely physical desire. The two slaveries in fact form a sort of natural counterpoise, the one to the other. When love becomes sufficient of a reality to hold the sex-passion as its powerful yet willing servant, the absurdity of Law will be at an end.

Surely it is not too much to suppose that a reasonable society will be capable of seeing these and other such things; that it will neither on the one hand submit to a cast-iron system depriving it of all grace and freedom of movement, nor on the other hand be in danger of falling into swamps of promiscuity; but that it will have the sense to recognise and establish the innumerable and delicate distinctions of relation which build up the fabric of a complex social organism. It will understand perhaps that sincere Love is, as we have said, a real fact and its own justification, and that however various or anomalous or unusual may be the circumstances and combinations under which it appears, it demands and has to be treated by society with the utmost respect and reverence—as a law unto itself, probably the deepest and most intimate law of human life, which only in the most exceptional cases, if at all, may public institutions venture to interfere with.

In all these matters it is surprising to-day what children we are—how we take the innumerable flowers and try to snip and shape all their petals and leaves to one sorry pattern, or how with a kind of grossness we snatch at and destroy in a few moments the bloom and beauty which are rightfully undying. Perhaps it will only be for a society more fully grown than ours to understand the wealth and variety of affectional possibilities which it has within itself, and the full enchantment of the many relations in which the romance of love by a tender discrimination and æsthetic continence is preserved for years and decades of years in, as it were, a state of ever-growing perfection.

Remarks and Notes

REMARKS AND NOTES

ON THE

EARLY STAR AND SEX WORSHIPS

THERE seems to be a certain propriety in the fact that two of the oldest and most universal cults have been the worship of the stars on the one hand, and the emblems of sex on the other. The stars, the most abstract, distant and universal of phenomena, symbols of changeless law and infinitude, before which human will and passion sink into death and nothingness; and sex, the very focus of passion and desire, the burning point of the will to live. Between these two poles the human mind has swayed since the eldest time.

With these earlier worships, too, the later religions have mingled in inextricable but not meaningless entanglement. The Passover, the greatest feast of the Jews, borrowed from the Egyptians, handed down to become the supreme festival of Christianity, and finally blending in the North of Europe with the worship of the Norse goddess Eastre, is as is well known closely connected with the celebration of the spring equinox and of the *passing over* of the sun from south to north of the equator—*i. e.*, from his winter depression to his summer dominion. The Sun, at the moment of passing the equinoctial point, stood 3,000 years ago in the Zodiacal constellation of the Ram or he-lamb. The Lamb, therefore, became the symbol of the young triumphant god. The Israelites (Exodus xii. 14.) were to smear their *doorways* (symbol of the passage from darkness to light) with the blood of the Lamb, in remembrance of the conflict of their god with the powers of darkness (the Egyptians). At an earlier date—owing to the precession of the equinoxes—the sun at the spring passage stood in the constellation of the Bull; so, in the older worships of Egypt and of Persia and of India, it was the Bull that was sacred and the symbol of the god. Moses is said to have abolished the worship of the Calf and to have consecrated the Lamb at the passover—and this appears to be a rude record of the fact that the astronomical changes were accompanied or followed by priestly changes of ceremonial. Certainly it is curious that in later Egyptian times the bull-headed god was deposed in favor of the ram-headed god Ammon; and that Christianity adopted the Lamb for the symbol of its Savior. Similarly, the Virgin Mary with the holy Child in her arms can be traced by lineal descent from the early Christian Church at Alexandria up through the later Egyptian times to Isis with the infant Horus, and thence to the constellation Virgo shining in the sky. In the representation of the Zodiac in the Temple of Denderah (in Egypt) the figure of Virgo is annotated by a smaller figure of Isis with Horus in her arms; and the Roman church fixed the celebration of Mary's assumption into glory at the very date (15th August) of the said constellation's disappearance from sight in the blaze of the solar rays, and her birth on the date (8th Sep.) of the same constellation's reappearance.*

The history of Israel reveals a long series of avowedly sexual and solar worships carried on alongside with that of Jehovah—worships of Baal, Ashtaroth, Nehushtan, the Host of Heaven, etc.—and if we are to credit the sacred record, Moses himself introduced the notoriously sexual Tree and Serpent worship (Numbers xxi. 9, and 2 Kings xviii. 4.); while Solomon, not without dramatic propriety, borrowed from the Phœnicians the two phallic pillars surmounted by pomegranate wreaths, called Jachin and Boaz, and placed them in front of his temple (1 Kings vii.

* These dates have shifted now by two or three weeks owing to the equinoctial precession.

21). The Cross itself (identical as a symbol with the *phallus* of the Greeks and the *lingam* of the East), the Fleur de Lys, which has the same signification, and the Crux Ansata, borrowed by the early Christians from Egypt and indicating the union of male and female, are woven and worked into the priestly vestments and altar-cloths of Christianity, just as the astronomical symbols are woven and worked into its Calendar, and both sets of symbols, astronomical and sexual, into the very construction of our Churches and Cathedrals. Jesus himself—so entangled is the worship of this greatest man with the earlier cults—is purported* to have been born like the other sungods, Bacchus, Apollo, Osiris, on the 25th day of December, the day of the sun's re-birth (*i. e.,* the first day which obviously lengthens after the 21st December—the day of the doubting apostle Thomas!) and to have died upon an instrument which, as already hinted, was ages before and all over the world held in reverence as a sexual symbol.

I have only touched the fringe of this great subject. The more it is examined into, the more remarkable is the mass of corroborative matter belonging to it. The conclusion towards which

* The date of his birth was not fixed till A. D. 531—when it was computed by a monkish astrologer.

one seems to be impelled is that these two great primitive ideas, sexual and astronomical, are likely to remain the poles of human emotion in the future, even as they have been in the past.

Some cynic has said that the two great ruling forces of mankind are Obscenity and Superstition. Put in a less paradoxical form, as that the two ruling forces are Sex and the belief in the Unseen, the saying may perhaps be accepted. To call the two Love and Faith (as Dr. Bucke does in his excellent book on *Man's Moral Nature*) is perhaps to run the risk of becoming *too* abstract and spiritual.

Roughly speaking we may say that the worship of Sex and Life characterised the Pagan races of Europe and Asia Minor anterior to Christianity, while the worship of Death and the Unseen has characterised Christianity. It remains for the modern nations to accept both Life and Death, both the Greek and the Hebrew elements, and all that these general terms denote, in a spirit of the fullest friendliness and sanity and fearlessness.

A curious part of all the old religions, Pagan or Christian—and this connects itself with the above—is Asceticism: that occasional instinct of voluntary and determined despite to the body and its senses. Even in the wildest races, rejoicing before all things in the consciousness of Life, we find festivals of fierce endurance and torments willingly undergone with a kind of savage glee;* and during the Christian centuries—monks, mystics, and world-spiting puritans—this instinct was sometimes exalted into the very first place of honor. I suppose it will have to be recognised—whatever absurd aberrations the tendency may have been liable to—that it is a basic thing in human nature, and as ineradicable in its way as the other equally necessary instinct towards Pleasure. To put it in another way, perhaps the ordinary Hedonism makes a mistake in failing to recognise the joy of Ascendancy, and (if it is not a "bull" to say so) the pleasure which lies in the denial of pleasure. In order to enjoy life one must be a master of life—for to be a slave to its inconsistencies can only mean torment; and in order to enjoy the senses one must be master of *them*. To dominate the actual world you must, like Archimedes, base your fulcrum somewhere beyond.

In such moods a man delights to feel his supremacy, not only over the beasts of the field, but over his own bodily and mental powers: no ordi-

* Note especially the ordeals through which the youth of so many savage races have had to pass before being admitted to manhood.

nary pleasure so great, but its reaction serves to throw out into relief this greater; no task so stern, but endurance is sterner; no pain so fierce but it wakes the soul to secret laughter. If there is something narrow in the creed of the ascetic on its negative side—that of denial—one cannot but feel that on its positive side, the establishment of authority and kingship, it has a real and vital meaning.

In another mood, however (equally undeniable and important), man acknowledges his delight in life, and gives the rein to his desires to chariot him to the extremest bounds of his kingdom. The kiss of the senses is beautiful beyond all and every abstraction; the touch of the sunlight, the glory of form and color, the magic of sweet sound, the joy of human embraces, the passion of sex—all so much the more perfect because they are as it were something divine made actual and realisable. In such a mood asceticism in any form seems the grossest impiety and folly, and the pursuit of the Unseen a mere abandonment of the world for its shadow.

Are not these two moods both necessary—the great rhythmical heart-beat, the *systole* and *diastole,* of the human soul? The one, a going forth and gathering of materials from all sources, the other an organising of them under the most perfect light, or rather (it may be said), a consumption of them to feed the most perfect flame; the one centrifugal, the other centripetal; the one individual, the other universal; and so forth—each required for the purposes of the other, and making the other possible?

Do we not want a truly experiential view of what may be called Religion—derived from the largest actual acquaintance with, and acceptance of, all the facts both of mundane and extra-mundane consciousness—neither (like some secularists) denying the one, nor (like some religionists) minimising or contemning the other? And is it not possible that in the early Star and Sex worships we have evidence of the attempt of the human mind to establish some such sane polarity?

NOTE

ON THE PRIMITIVE GROUP-MARRIAGE

ONE of the early forms of union among human beings appears to have been that of the *Group-Marriage,* which was an alliance between a group of men and a group of women. It had various forms, but rested in general on the fact that the women in primitive societies did not, on marriage, leave their parental habitation but remained there and were visited by the men—by one man first, who would come with presents of game, etc., from the chase, and would afterwards bring his "brothers" or friends. Thus in general a group of "brothers" would come into relation with a group of "sisters." In such a state of society, however, it is obvious that parentage would be very uncertain, and the terms brother and sister would not always have the stricter meanings which we give them. Such a group-marriage was the "Punalua" or "friend" marriage of Morgan's North American Indians; which is also supposed by Marx and Engels to have prevailed at an early time throughout Polynesia. See Lewis Morgan's

Ancient Society and Friederich Engels' *Ursprung der Familie.*

In later times the group-marriage became restricted in various directions, according to the genius of various races—marriage of cousins, for instance, being severely prohibited among some barbaric tribes, while among others *all* relatives (in the maternal line) were barred. Thus ultimately, in some quarters, sprang up a Pair-marriage; which however was only loosely defined; which had much of the old group-marriage lingering round it; and in which the children still belonged to the woman, and the descent was traced in the maternal line only.

Under these conditions of society the woman was comparatively well off. Remaining as she did in her own *gens* or clan and among her own relations, and the husband being as it were a visitor from the outside, she was by no means subject to him; in fact, in order to gain access, he had to make himself agreeable not only to her but to her own family! She had the disposal of the children; there was no danger of their being sequestrated to her husband; and whatever little property she had she could leave to them; to her was all the honor of ancestry. The husband on the other hand, even if he knew which his own children were, could see little of them, and could not leave his possessions to them without alienating those possessions from his clan—which the clan-customs would not permit. Thus in marriage he practically had to take the second place.

With the growth however of property and the sense of property, there came a time when the men could stand this state of affairs no longer, and insisted, violently at first, in carrying off the women and locating them in their own tents and among their own clans—a change rudely recorded probably in legends like the Rape of the Sabines, and in all the later customs of Marriage by Capture. And with this change marriage took on new forms. Women became the property of their husbands; they ceased to hold property of their own, in their children or in anything else; and descent was traced through the males only. In the Patriarchal system marriage was closely akin to slavery. Polygamy and Monogamy were the two resulting institutions.

Polyandry may perhaps be looked upon as a survival of the group-marriage in a special form adapted to warrior races; but—as Engels remarks—both Polygamy and Polyandry in any strict sense can only be regarded as exceptional institutions, since if they were general in any one country, that would imply a great preponderance of one sex over the other—unless indeed the two institutions existed side by side in the same country, which notoriously never happens. As a matter of fact in oriental countries Polygamy is confined to the rich, and is so to speak a luxury, within reach of the few only.

Thus it would appear that from the first, in oriental countries, the practices of polygamy and monogamy were intermixed. In Greece and Rome polygamy ceased to be recognised as an institution; though concubinage in one form or another remained. The Monogamic marriage became the legal institution; and the woman was handed over to the man as his chattel; was bought symbolically with his money, in the marriage ceremony; and had at first no more rights of her own than a chattel. In the later times, however, of the Roman Empire, with the institution of the dowry and the power granted to women of holding property, together with the great facilities of divorce allowed, the position of the Roman matron became much improved. And in modern European countries the monogamic institution seems to have passed or be passing through somewhat the same stages as in ancient Greece or Rome.

ON JEALOUSY

A GREAT disturber of the celestial order of Love is Jealousy—that brand of physical passion which carried over into the emotional regions of the mind will sometimes rage there like a burning fire. One may distinguish two kinds of jealousy, a natural and an artificial. The first arises perhaps from the real uniqueness of the relationship between two persons—at any rate as it appears to one of them—and the endeavor to stamp this uniqueness on the whole relationship, sexual and moral—especially on the sexual relationship. This kind of jealousy seems in a sense natural and normal, at any rate for a period; but when the personal relation between the two parties has been fully and confessedly established, and is no more endangered, the feeling does often I think (equally naturally) die away; and may do so quite well without damaging the intimacy and uniqueness of the alliance. This jealousy is felt with terrible keenness and intensity by lovers before the consummation of their passion, and perhaps for a year or two afterwards—though it may be protracted rather indefinitely in the case where the alliance, on one side at any rate, is not quite satisfactory.

The other kind of jealousy rests on the sense of property, and is the kind that is often felt by the average husband and wife long after honey-mooning days—by the husband not because of his especial devotion to his partner, but because he is furious at the idea of her disposing as she likes with what he considers *his property;* and by the wife because she is terrified at the thought that her matrimonial clothes-peg, from which depend all her worldly prospects, may vanish away or become the peg for another woman's clothes. This kind of jealousy is more especially the product of immediate social conditions, and is in that sense artificial. Though probably not quite so heart-rending as the other, it is often passionate enough, and lasts on indefinitely, like a chronic disease.

In early times, with the more communistic feeling of primitive societies, and with customs (like group-marriage) which allowed some latitude in sex-relation, jealousy though strong was not probably a very great force. But with the growth of individualism in life and in love, with the rise of the sense of property under civilisation and the accentuation of every personal feeling in what may be called the *cellular* state of society, the passion became one of fearful and convulsive power and fury; as is borne witness to by numberless dramas and poems and romances of the historical period. In the communism and humanism of the future, as the sense of property declines, and as Love rises more and more out of mere blind confusion with the sex-act, we may fairly hope that the artificial jealousy will disappear altogether, and that the other form of the passion will subside again into a comparatively reasonable human emotion.

ON THE FAMILY

A CHANGE somewhat similar to that in the position of Jealousy has taken place in the rôle of the Family during the progress of society into and through the period of civilisation. In the primitive human association the Family was large in extent, and in outline vague; the boundaries of kinship, in cases where the woman might have several husbands, or the husband several wives, were hard to trace; paternal feeling was little or not at all developed; and the whole institution rested on the maternal instinct of care for the young. In the middle societies of civilisation, and with monogamic arrangements, the Family grew exceedingly definite in form and circumscribed in extent. The growth of property and competition, and the cellular system of society, developed a kind of warfare between the units of which society was composed. These units were families. The essential communism and fraternity of society at large was dwarfed now and contracted into the limits of the family; and this institution acquired an extraordinary importance from the fact that it alone kept alive and showed in miniature (intensified by the darkness and chaos and warfare outside) the sacred fire of human fraternity. So great was this importance in fact that the Holy Family became one of the central religious conceptions of the civilised period, and it was commonly thought that society owed its existence to the Family—instead of, as was the case, the truth being the reverse, namely that the Family was the condensation of the principle which had previously existed, though diffused and unconscious, throughout society.

The third and future stage is of course easy to see—that is, the expansion again of the conception of the family *consciously* into the fraternity and communism of all society. It is obvious that as this takes place the family will once more lose its definition of outline and merge more and more again with the larger social groups in which it is embedded—but not into the old barbaric society in which the conception of human fellowship lay diffused and only dimly auroral, but into the newer society in which it shall be clear and all-illuminating as the sun.

Thus the Family institution in its present form, and as far as that form may be said to be artificial, will doubtless pass away. Nevertheless there remains, of course, and must remain, its natural or physiological basis—namely the actual physical relation of the parents to each other and to the child. One perhaps of the most valuable results of the Monogamic family institution under civilisation has been the development of the paternal feeling for the child, which in primitive society was so weak. To-day the love of man and wife for each other is riveted, as it never was in ancient days, by the tender beauty of the child-face, in which each parent sees with strange emotion his own features blended with the features of his loved one—the actual realisation of that union which the lovers so desired, and which yet so often seemed to them after all *not* consummated. The little prolongation of oneself, carrying in its eyes the star-look of another's love, and descending a stranger into the world to face a destiny all its own, touches the most personal and mortal-close feelings (as well as perhaps the most impersonal) of the heart. And while to-day this sight often reconciles husband and wife to the legal chains which perforce hold them together, in a Free Society, we may hope, it will more often be the sign and seal of a love which neither requires nor allows any kind of mechanical bond.

ON PREVENTIVE CHECKS TO POPULATION

THIS is no doubt a complex and difficult subject. Nature from far back time has provided in the most determined and obstinate way for the perpetuation of organic life, and has endowed animals, and even plants, with a strong sexual instinct. By natural selection this instinct tends, it would seem, to be accentuated; and in the higher animals and man it sometimes attains a pitch almost of ferocity. In civilised man this effect is further increased by the intensity of *consciousness*, which reflects desire on itself, as well as by collateral conditions of life and luxury.

In the animal and plant world generally, and up to the realm of Man, Nature appears to be perfectly lavish in the matter, and careless of the waste of seed and of life that may ensue, provided her object of race-propagation is attained; and naturally when the time arrives that Man, objecting to this waste, faces up to the problem, he finds it no easy one to solve.

And not only Man (the male) objects to lower Nature's method of producing superfluous individuals only to kill them off again in the struggle for existence; but Woman objects to being a mere machine for perpetual reproduction.

For meeting this difficulty, the only way commonly proposed—short of a continence and self-control almost amounting to total abstinence—is the adoption of some kind of artificial preventatives to conception. But it must be acknowledged that artificial checks to population are for the most part very unsatisfactory. Their uncertainty, their desperate matter-of-factness, so fatal to real feeling, the probability that they are in one way or another dangerous or harmful, and then their one-sidedness, since here—as so often in matters of sex—the man's satisfaction is largely at the cost of the woman: all these things are against them. One method however—that which consists in selecting, for sexual congress, a certain part of the woman's monthly cycle, can hardly be called artificial, and is altogether the least open to the objections cited. Its success truly is not absolutely certain, but is perhaps sufficiently nearly so for the general purpose of regulating the family; and if the method involves some self-control, it does not at any rate make an impracticable demand in that direction.

There is also another method which, while it may seem at first to demand considerable self-control, does really perhaps in the end yield fuller satisfaction than any. Late authors have pointed out that a distinction can and should be made between sexual intercourse for the definite purpose of race-propagation and sexual intercourse for simple union—that, in fact, the methods are different. Mrs. A. B. Stockham, in her little book "Karezza" (Mrs. A. B. Stockham, Alhambra, Cal.), dwells on this subject. She indicates that for the latter purpose, *i.e.*, union, there may be complete and indeed prolonged bodily conjunction; but the whole process being kept (by the use of a certain amount of physical control) on the emotional plane of endearment and affection, there need be no actual emission, and the final orgasm may be avoided. "Given abundant time and mutual reciprocity, the interchange becomes satisfactory and complete without emission or crisis by either party." The result of this is really a more complete *soul-union,* a strange and intoxicating exchange of life, and transmutation of elements. "The whole being of each is submerged in the other, and an exquisite exaltation experienced. . . In the course of an hour the physical tension subsides, the spiritual exaltation increases, and not uncommonly visions of transcendent life are seen, and consciousness of new powers experienced." This "gives to the sexual relation an office entirely distinct from the propagative act—it is a union on the affectional plane, but at the same time it is a preparation for best possible conditions for procreation."

The importance of this distinction of the generative act from the act of union or conjunction can hardly be overrated. The two things have hitherto been undifferentiated. Though it may not be easy at once to establish the mental and other conditions necessary for the latter, yet they can be established; and the result is an avoidance of waste, and a great economy of vital forces—on the one side a more profound, helpful and satisfying union, and on the other a greater energy for procreation, when that is desired. We cannot help thinking that it is along this line that the solution of the marriage and population problem will, in time, be found. The overhanging dread of undesired child-birth which so oppresses the life of many a young mother, will be removed; and marriage will be liberated at last from the tyranny of a brute need into the free and pleasurable exercise of a human and intelligent relationship.

Appendix

APPENDIX

PAGE 7.—"*Natural reticence.*"

SEX belongs to the Unconscious or universal-conscious regions of our nature (which is the meaning perhaps of Modesty), and will resume its place there some day. Meanwhile, having crept into the Conscious, it must for the time being be sincerely faced there.

PAGE 15.—"*To teach the child first, quite openly, its physical relation to its own mother.*"

"IT was not without much anxiety that I took the first step on the road I intended to explore alone. Chance favoured me. I was in Java, and amongst my servants was a dressmaker, married to the groom. This woman had a dear little baby with a velvety brown skin and bright black eyes, the admiration of my little daughter, whom I took with me to see mother and child, when the baby was a few days old. While she admired and petted it wonderingly, I said to her: 'This pretty little baby came out of Djahid like the beautiful butterfly came out of the chrysalis, it lay close to Djahid's heart, she made it, and kept it there till it grew. She loved it so much that she made it grow.' Lilly looked at me with her large, intelligent eyes in astonishment. 'Djahid is very happy to have this pretty baby. Djahid's blood made it strong while it lay close to her heart; now Djahid will give it milk, and make it strong, till it will grow as big as my Lilly. It made Djahid ill and made her suffer when it was born, but she soon got well, and she is so glad.' Lilly listened, very much interested, and when she got home, she told her father the story, forgetting nothing. But beyond that, she did not refer again to the matter, and soon forgot all about it. The birth of Djahid's second baby gave me the opportunity of repeating the little lesson. This time she asked some questions. I explained many things to the eager little listener, very simply, and told her that the mother kept the child within her, and took great care of it until it was old enough to endure the changes of temperature, etc., and showed her how a mother's joy and love made her forget her pain. The little creature, suddenly remembering that she must have given *her* mother pain, kissed me tenderly. That was a flower of love and gratitude, which it was my happiness to see develop on the fruitful soil of truth. . . . I analysed a flower, I pointed out to her the beauty of coloring, the gracefulness of shape, the tender shades, the difference between the parts composing the flowers. Gradually, I told her what these parts were called. I showed her the pollen, which clung like a beautiful golden powder to her little rosy fingers. I showed her through the microscope that this beautiful powder was composed of an infinite number of small grains. I made her examine the pistil more closely, and I showed her, at the end of the tube, the ovary, which I called a little house full of very tiny children. I showed her the pollen glued to the pistil, and I told her that when the pollen of one flower, carried away by the wind, or by the insects, fell on the pistil of another flower, the small grains died, and a tiny drop of moisture passed through the tube and entered into the little house where the tiny children dwelt; that these tiny children were like small eggs, that in each small egg there was an almost invisible opening, through which a little of the small drop passed; that when this drop of pollen mixed with some other wonderful power in the ovary, both joined together to give life, and the eggs developed and became grains or fruit. I have shown her flowers which had only a pistil and others which had only stamens. I said to her, smiling, that the pistils were like little mothers, and the stamens like little fathers of the fruit. . . . . Thus I sowed in this innocent heart and searching mind the seeds of that delicate science, which degenerates into obscenity, if the mother, through false shame, leaves the instruction of her child to its schoolfellows. Let my child ask me, if she likes, the much-dreaded question; I will only have to remind her of the botany lessons, simply adding, 'the same thing happens to human beings, with this difference, that what is done unconsciously by the plants, is done consciously by us; that in a properly arranged society one only unites one's self to the person one loves.' "—

Translated from "La Revendication des Droits Féminins," *Shafts, April, 1894*, p. 237.

PAGE 17.—*"The vulgarisation of love."*

"I HAVE found in my experience that those who seek to draw into the selfish confines of their own breasts the electric current of Love are withered by its force and passion. The energy degrades to sensualism if it has only the individual channel for expression. The sexual expression of Love is good and beautiful if normal, but it is not so infallible as the subtler intercourse of the soul and the affections, or so satisfying as a comradeship in work for Humanity, and a mental and spiritual affinity."—MIRIAM W. NICOL.

PAGE 26.—*"In the beauty and openness of their own bodies."*

"ALL the loves—if they be heroic and not purely animal, or what is called natural, and slaves to generation as instruments in some way of nature—have for object the divinity, and tend towards divine beauty, which first is communicated to, and shines in, souls; and from them or rather through them is communicated to bodies; whence it is that well-ordered affection loves the body or corporeal beauty, insomuch as it is an indication of beauty of spirit."—GIORDANO BRUNO, "Gli Eroici Furori" (dial. iii. 13), trans. by L. Williams.

"In Sparta the spectacle of the naked human body and the natural treatment of natural things were the best safeguard against the sexual excitement artificially produced by the modern plan of separating the sexes from the earliest childhood. The forms of one sex and the functions of its specific organs were no secret to the other. There was no possibility of trifling with ambiguities."—BEBEL'S "Woman," Bellamy Library, p. 70.

PAGE 28.—*Generation and nutrition.*

"IT is in the almost homogeneous fabrics of the cellular plants that we find the closest connection between the function of nutrition and that of reproduction; for every one of the vesicles which compose their fabric is endowed with the power of generating others similar to itself; and these may extend the parent structure or separate into new and distinct organisms. Hence it is scarcely possible to draw a line in these cases, between the nutrition of the individual, and the reproduction of the species."—W. B. CARPENTER, "Principles of Human Physiology," sec. 281.

PAGE 45.—*Secondary Differences between the Sexes.*

THE following are some of the points of difference given by H. Ellis in "Man and Woman" (Contemporary Science Series) :—

The average cranial capacity of men is greater than that of women (as would be expected from the general proportions of the sexes); but the *difference* in this respect between men and women is greater in the higher civilised races than in the lower and more primitive.

Evidence points on the whole to the *cerebellum* being, relatively, distinctly larger in women than in men.

Intellectually, women tend to the personal and concrete, men to the general and abstract.

Women endure pain, operations, etc., better than men, and show greater tenacity of life; men are superior in motor perfection, skill, and muscle. In delicacy of sense-perceptions the two sexes are about equal.

Women show in some respects a greater affectability than men, which is encouraged by their slight tendency to anæmia, by the greater development of their vaso-motor system, and by the periodicity of their functions. They are more hypnotic; the lower—that is, the more primitive and fundamental—nerve-centres preponderate and are more excitable; hysteria, ecstasy, and suggestibility, more marked.

Men show a greater tendency to race-variation than women; abnormalities of various kinds, idiots and geniuses, are commoner amongst males. Man represents the radical or experimental element in the life of the race.

Woman represents the conservative element. She remains nearer to the child, but for that very reason is in some respects more advanced than man, who, when he grows older, is "farther off from heaven than when he was a boy."

PAGE 55.—*Finesse in woman.*

THE method of attaining results by ruses (common among all the weaker lower animals) is so habitual among women that, as Lombroso and Ferrero remark, in woman deception is "almost physiological." . . . But to regard the caution and indirectness of women as due to innate wickedness, would, it need scarcely be said, be utterly irrational. It is inevitable, and results from the constitution of women, acting in the conditions under which they are generally placed. There is at present no country in the world, certainly no civilised country, in which a woman may safely state openly her wishes and desires, and proceed openly to seek their satisfaction."—HAVELOCK ELLIS, "Man and Woman," p. 174.

PAGE 60 (note).—*"The freedom of Woman must ultimately rest on the Communism of Society."*

"THE reproduction of the race is a social function, and we are compelled to conclude that it is the duty of the community, as a community, to provide for the child-bearer when in the exercise of her social function she is unable to provide for herself. The woman engaged in producing a new member, who may be a source of incalculable profit or danger to the whole community, cannot fail to be a source of the liveliest solicitude to everyone in the community, and it was a sane and beautiful instinct that found expression of old in the permission accorded to the pregnant woman to enter gardens and orchards, and freely help herself." —HAVELOCK ELLIS, Pamphlet on "Evolution in Sex," p. 15.

"She held it just that women should be so provided for, because the mothers of the community fulfill in the State as important and necessary a function as the men themselves do."—GRANT ALLEN, "The Woman Who Did," p. 73.

PAGE 61.—"*Menstrual troubles and disturbances.*"

THERE is little doubt that menstruation, as it occurs to-day in the vast majority of cases, is somehow pathological and out of the order of nature. In animals the periodic loss is so small as to be scarcely noticeable, and among primitive races of mankind it is as a rule markedly less than among the higher and later races. We may therefore suppose that its present excess is attributable to certain conditions of life which have prevailed for a number of centuries, and which have continuously acted to bring about a feverish disposition of the sexual apparatus, and an hereditary tendency to recurrent manifestations of a diseased character. Among conditions of life which in all probability *would* act in this way may be counted (1) the indoor life and occupations of women, leading to degeneration of the neuro-muscular system, weakness, and inflammability; (2) the heightening of the sex-passion in both men and women with the increase of luxury and artificialism in life; (3) the subjection of the woman to the unrestrained use and even abuse of the man, which inevitably took place as soon as she—with the changes in the old tribal life—became his chattel and slave; and which has continued practically ever since. These three causes acting together over so long a period may well seem sufficient to have induced a morbid and excessive habit in the female organism; and if so we may hope that with their removal the excess itself and a vast amount of concomitant human misery and waste of life-power will disappear.

PAGE 66.—*"Natural desires."*

"ALTHOUGH I agree with Malthus as to the value of virtuous abstinence, the sad conviction is forced upon me as a physician that the chaste morality of women—which though it is certainly a high virtue in our modern states is none the less a crime against nature—not infrequently revenges itself in the cruelest forms of disease."—DR. HEGERISCH, translator of Malthus.

PAGE 69.—*"They must learn to fight."*

"WOMEN have as little hope from men as workmen from the middle classes."—BEBEL, "Woman," p. 72.

PAGE 71.—*"Sexual selection exercised by the female."*

"HUNGER—that is to say, what we call economic causes—has, because it is the more widespread and constant, though not necessarily the more imperious instinct, produced nearly all the great zoological revolutions. . . . Yet love has, in the form of sexual selection, even before we reach the vertebrates, moulded races to the *ideal* of the female; and reproduction is always the chief end of nutrition which hunger waits on, the supreme aim of life everywhere."—"Evolution in Sex," p. 12.

PAGE 77.—"*The features of a grander type.*"

"TOWARDS the Future I look and see a greater race to come—of beautiful women, athletic, free, able in mind and logic, great in love and maternal instincts, unashamed of their bodies and the sexual parts of them, calm in nerve, and with a chronic recognition of Spiritual qualities—a race of men, gentle, strong, courageous, continent, affectionate, unselfish, large in body and mind, full of pluck and brawn, able to suffer, clean and honest in their animal necessities, self-confident, with no king or overseer."—MIRIAM WHEELER NICOL.

PAGE 83.—"*The search for a fitting mate.*"

"WITH the disappearance of the artificial barriers in the way of friendship between the sexes, and of the economic motive to sexual relationships—which are perhaps the two chief forces now tending to produce promiscuous sexual intercourse, whether dignified or not with the name of marriage—men and women will be free to engage, unhampered, in the search, so complicated in a highly civilised condition of society, for a fitting mate."—"Evolution in Sex," p. 13.

PAGE 84—(note).—*Desire of congress less strong in woman.*

"I WILL mention here that from various late sources of information I conclude that *sexual insensibility* in women is much commoner than usually assumed. Of course I mean by this, insensibility as from the sexual standpoint: of the sense of pleasure and satisfaction in congress, as well as the desire for congress. This desire is much less frequent in woman than generally supposed. But the soul-side of love on the other hand is often more prominent in females than in males." —A. MOLL, "Conträre Sexual-empfindung," 2nd edn., p. 325.

PAGE 89.—*"In this serf-life their very natures have been blunted."*

"NOT so the wife; however brutal a tyrant she may be chained to . . . he can claim from her and enforce the lowest degradation of a human being, that of being made the instrument of an animal function contrary to her inclinations. . . . No amount of ill-usage, without adultery superadded, will in England free a wife from her tormentor." — MILL'S "Subjection of Women," 1869.

Clitheroe Case, 1891.—After the refusal of the wife to cohabit, the husband said: "I therefore *took* my wife, and have since detained her in my house, using no more force or restraint than necessary to take her and keep her."

The Lord Chancellor said, "I am of opinion that no such right or power exists in law"—and ordered the lady to be restored to her liberty.—"Woman Free," by ELLIS ETHELMER, p. 144.

PAGE 102.—*The Monogamic Marriage.*

"IN attempting to estimate the moral worth of a people, a race, or a civilisation, we are much more enlightened by the position given to woman than by the legal type of the conjugal union. This type, besides, is usually more apparent than real. In many civilisations, both dead and living, legal monogamy has for its chief object the regulation of succession and the division of property."—LETOURNEAU, "Evolution of Marriage," p. 186.

Conjugal unions among the animals.—"Among many of the animal species the sexual union induces a durable association, having for its object the rearing of young. In nobility, delicacy, and devotion these unions do not yield precedence to any human unions."—*Ibid.*, p. 19.

"It is especially interesting to study the various modes of conjugal and familial association among birds. This may be easily inferred from the ardour, the variety and delicacy they bring to their amours. . . . There are some birds absolutely fickle and even debauched—as, for example, the little American starling (*Icterus pecoris*), which changes its female from day to day. . . . Other species, while they have renounced promiscuity, are still determined polygamists. The gallinaceae are particularly addicted to this form of conjugal union, which is so common in fact with mankind, even when highly civilised and boasting of their practice of monogamy. Our barndoor cock, vain and sensual, courageous and jealous, is a perfect type of the polygamous bird." . . . .—*Ibid.*, p. 26.

"Nearly all the rapacious animals, even the stupid vultures, are monogamous. The conjugal union of the bald-headed eagle appears even to last till the death of one of the partners." . . . .

"With the female Illinois parrot (*Psittacus pertinax*) widowhood and death are synonymous, a circumstance rare enough in the human species, yet of which the birds give us more than one example. When, after some years of conjugal life, a Wheat-ear happens to die, his companion hardly survives him a month."—*Ibid.*, p. 27.

"Bad fathers are rare among birds. Often on the contrary the male rivals the female in love for the young; he guards and feeds her during incubation, and sometimes even sits on the eggs with her. The carrier pigeon feeds his female while she is sitting; the Canadian goose and the crow do the same; more than that, the latter takes his companion's place at times, to give her some relaxation. The blue marten behaves in the same manner. Among many species male and female combine their efforts without distinction of sex;

they sit in turn, and the one who is free takes the duty of feeding the one who is occupied. This is the custom of the black-coated gull, the booby of Bassan, the great blue heron, and of the black vulture."—*Ibid.*, p. 30.

"In regard to mammals, there is no strict relation between the degree of intellectual development and the form of sexual union. The carnivorous animals often live in couples; but this is not an absolute rule, for the South African lion is frequently accompanied by four or five females. Bears, weasels, whales, etc., generally go in couples. Sometimes species that are very nearly allied have different conjugal customs; thus the white-cheeked peccary lives in troops, whilst the white-ringed peccary lives in couples. There is the same diversity in the habits of monkeys. Some are polygamous and other monogamous. The Wanderoo (*Macacus Silenus*) of India has only one female and is faithful to her until death. The *Cebus Capucinus,* on the contrary, is polygamous."—*Ibid.*, p. 33.

PAGE 108.—"*The destinies of a life-time.*"

"UNLIKE the Catholic Church in its dealings with novices, Society demands [in marriage] the ring, the parchment, and the vow as a *preliminary* to the knowledge and experience; hence adulteries, the divorce court, home-prisons, and the increase of cant and pruriency in the community. Unless a woman knows what a man's body is like, with its virile needs, and realises to the full her own adult necessities, how is it possible that she can have the faintest conception as to whether the romantic passionate impulse a man awakens in her is the trinity of love, trust and reverence, which alone lays the foundation of real marriage?"—EDITH M. ELLIS, "A Noviciate for Marriage," p. 13.

PAGE 114.—*"Contracts of some kind will still be made."*

"IT is therefore probable that a future more or less distant will inaugurate the régime of monogamic unions, freely contracted, and, at need, freely dissolved by simple mutual consent, as is already the case with divorces in various European countries—at Geneva, in Belgium, in Roumania, etc., and with separation in Italy. In these divorces of the future, the community will only intervene in order to safeguard that which is of vital interest to it—the fate and the education of the children. But this evolution in the manner of understanding and practising marriage will operate slowly, for it supposes an entire corresponding revolution in public opinion; moreover, it requires as a corollary profound modifications in the social organism."—LETOURNEAU, "Evolution of Marriage," p. 358.

"The antique morals which hold woman as a servile property belonging to her husband still live in many minds. They will be extinguished by degrees. The matrimonial contract will end by being the same kind of contract as any other, freely accepted, freely maintained, freely dissolved; but where constraint has disappeared deception becomes an unworthy offence. Such will be the opinion of a future humanity, more elevated morally than ours. Doubtless it will no longer have any tender indulgence for conveniently dissimulated adultery, but, on the other hand, it will no longer excuse the avenging husband."—*Ibid.*, p. 148.

PAGE 116.—*Contracts preliminary to a permanent alliance.*

"THE custom of hand-fasting, rare now anywhere else, still prevails to some extent in Iceland. A man and woman contract to live together for a year. If at the end of the year the parties agree thereto, they are married; if not, they separate without stigma on either side. The contract may be made conditionally binding from the first. It may bind the parties to marry in the event of issue, or in the event of no issue, as the case may be."—PROF. MAVOR, "Iceland: Some sociological and other notes." Proceedings Philosophical Society, Glasgow, 1890-91.

PAGE 122.—*The Intermediate Sex.*

"URNING men and women, on whose book of life Nature has written her new word which sounds so strange to us, bear such storm and stress within them, such ferment and fluctuation, so much complex material having its outlet only towards the future; their individualities are so rich and many-sided, and withal so little understood, that it is impossible to characterise them adequately in a few sentences."—OTTO DE JOUX.

PAGE 147.—*A certain amount of animalism.*

"THE Saviours of this, as of every corrupt and stupid generation, must feel the pulse of the adulterer as well as that of his victim, and stand clear-eyed and honest as pioneers of the new sexual renaissance, which will probably combine a healthy temperate animalism with Browning's vision of that rare mating when soul lies by soul."—EDITH M. ELLIS, "A Noviciate for Marriage," p. 4.

"She gave him comprehension of the meaning of love: a word in many mouths, not often explained. With her, wound in his idea of her, he perceived it to signify a new start in our existence, a finer shoot of the tree stoutly planted in good gross earth; the senses running their live sap, and the minds companioned, and the spirits made one by the whole-natured conjunction. In sooth, a happy prospect for the sons and daughters of Earth, divinely indicating more than happiness: the speeding of us, compact of what we are, between the ascetic rocks and the sensual whirlpools, to the creation of certain nobler races, now very dimly imagined."—GEORGE MEREDITH'S "Diana of the Crossways," ch. 37.